MEXICO AND THE UNITED STATES TODAY

Mexico AND THE United States Today
ISSUES BETWEEN NEIGHBORS

MARGARET FLESHER
RIBAROFF

Franklin Watts
New York London An Impact Book
Toronto Sydney

1985

Map by Vantage Art, Inc.
Photographs courtesy of:
UPI/Bettmann Archive:
pp. 4, 39, 44, 64, 80, 89;
The Bettmann Archive: pp. 7, 17, 24;
AP/Wide World: p. 51.

Library of Congress Cataloging in Publication Data
Ribaroff, Margaret Flesher.
Mexico and the United States today.
(An Impact book)
Bibliography: p.
Includes index.
Summary: Discusses the relationship between Mexico and the United States, their common interests and differences, and the issues between them.
1. United States—Foreign relations—Mexico—Juvenile literature. 2. Mexico—Foreign relations—United States—Juvenile literature. [1. United States—Foreign relations—Mexico. 2. Mexico—Foreign relations—United States] I. Title.
E183.8.M6R49 1985   327.73072   84-22115
ISBN 0-531-04757-1

Copyright © 1985 by Margaret Flesher Ribaroff
All rights reserved
Printed in the United States of America
6 5 4 3 2 1

CONTENTS

Chapter One
Neighbors 1

Chapter Two
The View from Mexico 6

Chapter Three
The United States Perspective 22

Chapter Four
From Boom to Bust 37

Chapter Five
Between Austerity and Recovery 48

Chapter Six
The Indocumentados 62

Chapter Seven
Searching for Peace in Central America 79

Chapter Eight
What Lies Ahead? 95

For Further Reading 99

Index 101

*To Alex,
for his help and encouragement*

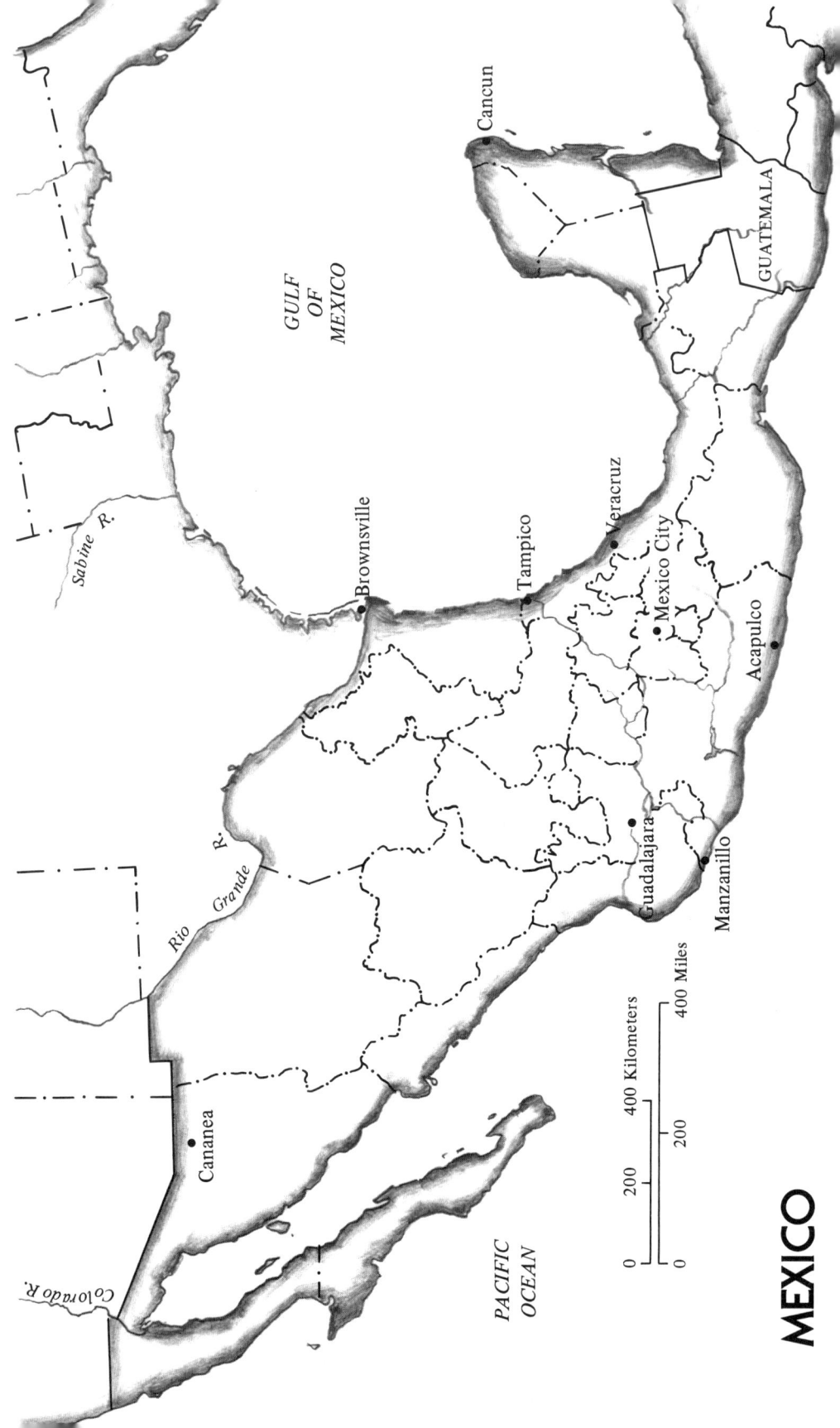

NEIGHBORS

Miguel de la Madrid Hurtado was sworn in as president of Mexico on December 1, 1982. In accepting the red, green, and white sash that symbolizes presidential power, Mr. de la Madrid undertook to govern Mexico until 1988—a six-year period that promises to be the most critical Mexico has faced in fifty years. During the months leading up to the inauguration, Mexico had sunk to the depths of an economic crisis so severe that it threatened the very foundations of the nation.

Almost half the labor force was either unemployed or unable to earn an adequate living; inflation was raging at almost 100 percent; Mexico owed more than $80 billion to foreign banks; and the price of oil, on which Mexico had based its hopes for prosperity, was in sharp decline, drastically reducing Mexico's income. In order to reduce the government's expenditures, officials had cut long-standing subsidies on gasoline and essential foods such as *tortillas* and bread. The new president's evaluation of the situation was not overstated. "We are in an emergency," he said in his inaugural speech.

The first order of business for the new administration was to try to set Mexico on the road to economic recovery and restore the confidence of both citizens and foreign investors in the country's future. But even without the burden of financial crisis, President de la Madrid faced a staggering array of problems at home and abroad.

Mexico has long had one of the highest birth rates in Latin America, and even though it has been reduced from 3 percent to 2.5 percent in the years since 1970, the pressures of a rapidly increasing population on Mexico's resources are enormous. The demand for jobs, food, housing, and health care will continue to expand as the population grows.

A companion problem is the severe inequality in the distribution of Mexico's wealth. The extremes of rich and poor are among the greatest in Latin America, and the difference between rural and urban standards of living is enormous.

President de la Madrid also faces challenges in the international arena. Mexico was an early supporter of the Sandinista army that overthrew the dictatorship of Anastasio Somoza Debayle in Nicaragua in 1979 and has supported the guerrillas who oppose the government in El Salvador. But political disturbances in Guatemala, on Mexico's southern border, have quite literally brought home the crisis created by revolutionary movements in Central America. Mexican leaders publicly reject the suggestion that the violence in the region might spill over into their country, but the potential for unrest increases as the quality of life diminishes for Mexico's poor and middle class.

As he seeks solutions to Mexico's domestic and regional problems, President de la Madrid faces the challenging task of working toward a mutually acceptable relationship with the United States. There is hardly an area of public policy in Mexico that is not affected in some way by that country's interaction with the United States. At the same time, Mexico is extremely important to the United States—as a market for U.S. exports, as a supplier of oil and natural gas, and as a power in the Western Hemisphere and in the Third World. In addition, many of Mexico's social problems directly affect the United States when they contribute to the rising tide of unemployed Mexican workers who illegally cross the border seeking jobs.

The relationship between Mexico and the United States in the 1980s is as complex as the issues that simultaneously divide and unite the two countries. Differences in history, culture, politics, and economic development linger in the background every time representatives of Mexico and the United States sit down to discuss a matter of joint interest, be it an agreement on fishing rights or the future of Central America.

Nevertheless, the two countries continue to talk, to negotiate, to look for answers to difficult questions. The United States embassy in Mexico City is the largest of all its embassies because of the extensive business carried out by government agencies dealing with health, culture, tourism, aviation, narcotics control, environmental protection, science and technology, and cooperation between customs offices. Representatives from the Mexican and United States Congresses meet regularly, and contacts between educators and business people are frequent. Governors from states on both sides of the border are increasingly working together to find solutions to such issues as water use and environmental pollution that affect their citizens.

A sign of the importance both countries attach to their relations is the tradition that presidents-elect from each country meet their counterparts before they take office. When President-elect Miguel de la Madrid met with Ronald Reagan in October 1982, he summed up the relationship between the two countries:

> Our friendship is founded on respect and dignity. Good friends do not always think alike, but they place understanding and comprehension above their differences.

This book is about Mexico and the United States—about the common interests that unite them and the differences that separate them. Today these neighboring countries approach each other with vastly different economic and political points of view, with different interpretations of

their common history, and different views of what best serves the interests of their people. The chapters that follow will examine the ways in which these varying perspectives influence three major issues between the countries: maintaining a profitable trading partnership, resolving the dilemma of undocumented workers in the United States, and reconciling deep-seated differences over political change in Central America.

First, however, it is important to look back to earlier times, to consider the origins of some of the attitudes that shape Mexico–United States relations today.

The past meets the present.
U.S. President Ronald Reagan
and Mexico's then President-elect
Miguel de la Madrid confer under
a statue of Benito Juarez in Tijuana.

CHAPTER

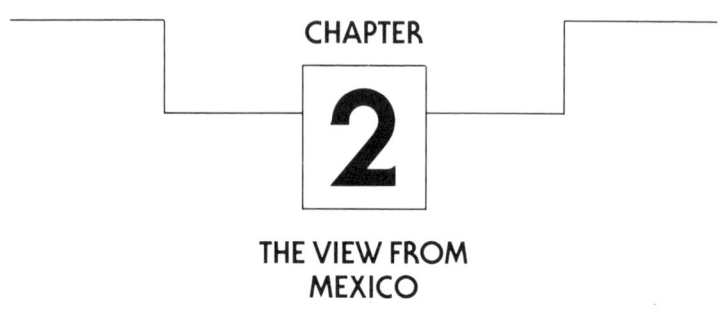

THE VIEW FROM MEXICO

The two-thousand-mile border between Mexico and the United States separates two nations whose origins marked them from the start for different paths in the world. Almost a century before English settlers began arriving in North America, Spanish *conquistadores* had established a foothold in New Spain, today's Mexico. Although the *conquistadores* never found the cities of gold that lured them to conquer Mexico's large Indian population, they did open the door to three hundred years of Spanish rule that shaped the culture of the nation.

Unlike the North American colonists, who destroyed the native people and drove them from their lands, the Spaniards recognized in the Indians of Mexico a valuable source of labor for the farms and mines they sought to establish. Additionally, the devout Spaniards saw in the Indians an opportunity to gain converts to the Catholic faith, and conversion became one of the chief goals of the conquest of Mexico. The priests who followed the *conquistadores* to New Spain were soon teaching the Indians Spanish in order to instruct them in the principles of Christianity, establishing Spanish as the official language of the country and Catholicism as its religion.

The Spanish colonial period also saw the beginning of a class structure that has persisted in Mexican society to the present day. At the top of this system was a small

Cortez and his conquistadores *captured the capital city of Mexico.*

upper class of *criollos*, originally Spaniards who owned and controlled the land, the silver mines, the financial institutions, and the government of the province. At the wide base of the system, which is often described as a pyramid, were the Indians who formed the underclass of laborers in the enterprises of the *criollos*. As the Spaniards and their descendants began to intermarry with the Indians, a new, distinctly American class was born. These were the *mestizos*, whose mixed ancestry gave them a place in the middle of the social pyramid. A small class at first, the *mestizos* are now the largest group in Mexican society and today form the basis of the country's growing middle class.

As important as the Spanish influence was in the development of Mexico's society and culure, it is not the only element in Mexico's past. In many ways Spanish colonial life was superimposed on a succession of Indian cultures that had dominated Mexico for 1,500 years. The Spaniards, for example, built their capital, Mexico City, on the site of the Aztec city of Tenochtitlán, and elements of the Indians' traditional worship were absorbed in the Catholic ritual to produce a uniquely Mexican "folk" Catholicism. This layering and mingling of cultures have given Mexico a strong sense of antiquity in its national heritage.

Mexico's concern with the past has influenced its attitude toward the United States for well over a century, for the Mexican people have kept alive vivid memories of arrogance and injustice, of military aggression and economic dominance at the hands of the United States. The actions of the United States in three particular periods are remembered with anger and sorrow and therefore have special significance even today in Mexico's relations with its neighbor. These three periods are the War of 1846-48, in which Mexico lost much of its territory to the United States; the regime of Porfirio Díaz, when in the early twentieth century the United States, with other foreign countries, controlled most of the economic activity in Mexico; and the Mexican Revolution of 1911-17, which overthrew Díaz and established the basis for modern Mexico.

THE WAR OF 1846–48

When Mexico won its independence from Spain in 1821, it inherited the problem of controlling a territory that reached from present-day California as far east as Texas and stretched southward to Mexico's present border with Guatemala. For centuries, even long before the Spaniards arrived, Mexico's economic activity and cultural and political life had been concentrated in the broad, fertile central plateau where the important cities of Guadalajara and Mexico City are located. To the north, by contrast, much of the land was rugged and barren, and in some areas tribes of nomadic Indians vigorously discouraged white settlers from encroaching on their land. Aside from a few coastal villages in California and scattered mission settlements in the interior, the distant northern provinces of Mexico had attracted few immigrants.

Quite the opposite was true in the United States of the 1820s. North Americans were on the move westward, opening new land to settlement and carrying their values and culture far from the established centers of power along the Atlantic seaboard. Many of these pioneers were drawn to the northern Mexican province of Texas by the promise of cheap land and a large measure of self-government. By 1835, approximately 20,000 North Americans were living in Texas, compared with only 7,800 Mexicans. For the most part, these colonists thought of themselves as Americans. They spoke English, retained their Protestant faith, and traded with their countrymen in the United States. When Mexico sought to end immigration to Texas and bring the province firmly under its control, the Texans rebelled, declaring themselves independent of Mexico on March 2, 1836. In the brief, bloody conflict that followed, the Texans defeated the militarily superior Mexicans only through timely support of men and supplies from the United States.

The United States had long had an eye on Texas and had even attempted unsuccessfully to buy the province from Mexico. After Texas became independent, the United States hoped to annex the new republic, making it eligible for statehood.

Mexico, meanwhile, never recognized the independent Texas and continued to consider the territory its own. Not surprisingly, Mexico viewed any move by the United States to annex Texas an act of war. When the Texas Congress voted to join the United States in June 1845, Mexico broke off diplomatic relations with the United States.

By the following spring several events had made war between Mexico and the United States inevitable. Texas had officially become the twenty-eighth state in the Union, and President James K. Polk had ordered a naval blockade of the mouth of the Rio Grande (known in Mexico as the Río Bravo del Norte). Polk had also sent General Zachary Taylor to occupy territory on the north bank of the Rio Grande—a region whose ownership had been sharply disputed between Mexico and Texas. In response to this action, Mexico, despite an upheaval in its government, marshaled its troops to drive out the United States forces. On May 11, 1846, President Polk asked Congress to declare war on Mexico.

When the war began, the Mexican army was judged to be both larger and more powerful than the United States forces. But eventually the Mexican forces fell victim to the country's lack of political leadership. In the end, the United States troops proved better disciplined, better equipped, and more politically unified in their pursuit of victory.

The United States cavalry faced little opposition in the northern provinces and in the central region of Mexico. In the south, however, the forces led by General Winfield Scott inflicted brutal damage. The port city of Veracruz fell after a ferocious bombardment that took the lives of women and children as well as soldiers, and General Scott's troops then marched on Mexico City. There in the final battle of the war, they successfully attacked Chapultepec Castle, a fortification defended by regular soldiers and by the young cadets of the Military Academy. The heroism of the cadets in this battle became legend in Mexico, and today these *Niños Héroes* are honored by a monument at the entrance of Chapultepec Park in Mexico City.

The results of the war reflected the imbalance between the power of Mexico and that of the United States. Under the terms of the Treaty of Guadalupe Hidalgo, which ended the hostilities, the boundary between the two countries was set at the Rio Grande as far as the Texas town of El Paso, and westward from there to the Pacific Ocean.* Mexico in return received $18,250,000 in compensation for a war that had cost the country 50,000 lives and half its territory.

The legacy of the war was bitterness toward the United States on the part of almost all Mexicans. People who had once admired the United States for its high political ideals, its representative government, and its drive for economic progress now decried "Yankee imperialism." The humiliation of defeat at the hands of the United States, however, had the effect of giving the people a common enemy to oppose. This sense of unity against the "colossus of the North" was the beginning of Mexican nationalism. The fact that Mexico's nationalist spirit was nourished from the start by anti-American sentiment became a crucial element in its relations with the United States. Some sixty years after the Treaty of Guadalupe Hidalgo, Mexicans found their nationalism a rallying point against renewed United States intervention in their country. This time, the intervention was not military but economic and political.

*In 1854 James Gadsden paid Mexico $10 million for almost 30,000 square miles of land in order to build a railroad through the Gila River valley in what are now the states of Arizona and New Mexico. This agreement gave the border between the United States and Mexico its present shape.

THE PORFIRIATO: 1876-1911

The middle decades of the nineteenth century were marked in Mexico by intense conflict between the opposing forces of conservatism and liberalism. This period saw, in turn, the imposition of a European monarch, the Emperor Maximilian, as the head of the government, and the establishment of a constitutional government under Benito Juárez, the hero of Mexican liberalism. But if Juárez began to move his country toward political stability and economic development, it fell to one of his generals, Porfirio Díaz, to continue Mexico's industrial progress into the twentieth century. Díaz's regime, often called "The Porfiriato" after the man who ruled Mexico as a virtual dictator for thirty-five years, is the second period in which United States actions in Mexico left a memory of callous disregard for the sensitivities and well-being of its inhabitants.

When Porfirio Díaz seized power in a military coup in 1876, he determined to develop his country's bountiful resources and bring Mexico into the industrial age. "Order and Progress" was the motto of the Díaz government. To gain the large sums of money necessary to build a modern, industrialized nation, Díaz turned outward to foreign investors. After 1900 he looked particularly to the United States, where a period of economic expansion had given successful entrepreneurs surplus profits to invest abroad.

Under a system of concessions—permits from the Mexican government to engage in various businesses—United States businessmen built railroads, developed copper mines, and established large-scale agricultural enterprises producing cattle, sugar, coffee, rubber, and henequin fiber for export. United States investment in Mexico between 1902 and 1911 was three times greater than all other foreign investment combined, and twice as much as the Mexicans' own investment in their country. This dominant position in Mexico's economy gave the

United States a great deal of political power which it used to ensure the continuation of the Díaz regime.

For the Mexican people, the quality of life under the Porfiriato depended very much on one's position in society. For the upper classes—the wealthy landowners called *hacendados* who controlled almost all the land as well as banks and many businesses—economic development brought prosperity and power. They eagerly affected the fashions and attitudes of the foreigners whose money supported their lavish entertainments, their prestigious clubs, and their children's education at the best private schools in Europe and the United States. The material benefits of industrialization, however, were slow to filter down to those lower on Mexico's social pyramid.

The process of industrialization had created a working class which by 1910 numbered about 800,000. For these men and women, working conditions and living standards were often appalling. Even for the small group of skilled workers, technicians, and engineers employed by U.S.-owned companies, wages were lower than those paid to American workers. And advancement for Mexican workers was impossible because all managerial positions were held by North Americans. This was the case at William L. Greene's copper mine in Cananea, a town in northern Sonora, near the Arizona border.

More than 5,000 Mexicans were employed at the Cananea mine, along with about 2,000 North Americans. In 1906, the Mexicans organized a strike to protest the discrimination they experienced in wages and opportunities. Their demands were simple and just: equal wages with their North American counterparts; improved opportunities for promotion; an eight-hour workday. During the course of the strike, a throng of unarmed Mexican workers pushed through a locked gate into a yard where they were met by gunshots from Americans inside. Thirty Mexicans and two American managers died in the melee.

The aftermath of this incident demonstrated the

influence of American investors in Mexico at the time. In the atmosphere of tension that followed the violence at Cananea, William Greene requested that a force of Arizona Rangers cross the border to keep the peace in the Mexican town. The action was quietly allowed by the governor of Sonora, even though the Rangers' presence was a clear violation of Mexico's territory. By calling in the Arizona Rangers to restore calm in what should have been a problem for Mexican law enforcers, Greene demonstrated that economic power could command the power to control political decisions.

Images such as this remain in the Mexican consciousness and contribute today to a deep-seated fear that the United States, with its wealth and advanced technology, might again come to dominate the Mexican economy. Although Mexican laws now prevent foreigners from controlling Mexican corporations and guarantee Mexican ownership of mineral resources such as oil and copper, the economic power of the United States is still perceived by Mexicans as a potential threat.

The threat is all the greater when it carries the possibility of either political or military intervention by the stronger nation to protect the interests of its citizens. Today the idea that the United States might use military force against Mexico to protect its economic interests may seem preposterous to most North Americans, but not to many Mexicans who remember not only the era of Porfirio Díaz, but also United States actions during the turbulent years of the Mexican Revolution of 1911–17.

"MEXICO FOR THE MEXICANS": THE REVOLUTION OF 1911–17

By 1910 the thirty-four-year regime of Porfirio Díaz was in trouble. Mexican workers were growing increasingly nationalistic in their demands for equal pay and opportunity in U.S.-owned industries, especially in the northern border states. Even the prosperous *hacendados* were weary of seeing their land—the basis of their wealth—

fall into the hands of North American cattle ranchers and agricultural exporters. Aside from these large foreign-owned agricultural businesses, Díaz had neglected the agricultural side of Mexico's economy in his drive to create an industrial society. The inevitable result was that Mexico's large population of peasants had received virtually none of the benefits of modernization. Many peasants, particularly those who owned no land of their own but worked on the large *haciendas,* provided a willing army for leaders such as Emiliano Zapata and Pancho Villa.

It was, however, Mexico's emerging middle class—lawyers, teachers, civil servants, engineers, technicians, and skilled workers—who perhaps felt most acutely that they were being denied the full fruits of economic progress and participation in the political process. And, more significantly, it was this group that had the education, the organizational abilities, and the financial resources to overthrow the eighty-year-old Porfirio Díaz. Led by Francisco I. Madero, a lawyer and member of a prominent family in Coahuila, the opposition to Díaz gathered strength in late 1910. Under a banner of nationalism, the middle classes united with workers and many landowners to proclaim "Mexico for the Mexicans!" In May 1911, Díaz's federal army was defeated by rebel forces at Ciudad Juárez on the Texas border. Shortly afterward, Díaz resigned as president and went into exile in Spain. His departure, however, was only the beginning of six years of bitter civil war among several factions seeking to fill the vacuum of effective leadership.

During this period, the United States government, not surprisingly, was alarmed by the events that were unfolding in the country on its southern border. By 1913, Francisco Madero's efforts to establish a moderate, democratic government had failed. Madero himself had been assassinated and Mexico was once again governed by a dictator, General Victoriano Huerta. Because Huerta had seized power illegally, the United States president, Woodrow Wilson, did not want to recognize his government and even tried to persuade Huerta to step down from the presidency. When this effort failed, Wilson found an excuse to escalate a minor incident into a major conflict—the seizure of the Mexican port of Veracruz.

In April 1914, United States warships were cruising off the Mexican coast, near the port of Tampico. When several sailors went ashore at Tampico to purchase gasoline, they were arrested when they mistakenly walked into a restricted area on the dock. The sailors were released almost immediately, and an official apology was made to the commander of the United States naval forces in the region. The commander, however, insisted on a more formal apology. With President Wilson's support, he insisted that the Mexicans offer a twenty-one-gun salute to an American flag flying on their shore. After some consideration, President Huerta agreed, providing the Americans would salute the Mexican flag in the same manner, a gesture that would have amounted to acceptance of the Huerta government. Wilson's response was to order the U.S. fleet to the Gulf of Mexico. To make matters worse, when tensions were running high, Wilson received word that a German merchant ship was approaching the port of Veracruz with arms for Huerta's forces. To forestall delivery of the weapons, Wilson ordered the U.S. troops to occupy Veracruz, and many Mexicans died defending their city.

Throughout Mexico reaction to the United States intervention was swift and harsh. American businesses were plundered and American flags burned. Tourists and American residents alike were threatened. Wilson's action led to Huerta's eventual downfall, earning the United States added criticism for meddling in Mexico's political affairs. But Veracruz was not the end of U.S. military interference in the Mexican Revolution.

The second time the United States forces intervened was in pursuit of the legendary bandit and folk hero, Pancho Villa. In the waning days of Mexico's civil war, in 1916, Pancho Villa commanded an enormous army of rebels in the northern Mexican state of Chihuahua and aspired to lead the entire country as spokesman for the common people. He was opposed by another peasant

The famed bandit Pancho Villa gallops alongside his troops during the Mexican Revolution.

army led by Emiliano Zapata in the south, and by the moderate faction of Venustiano Carranza. Villa had long hoped to win the backing of the United States in this three-way struggle for political supremacy, but in 1916 President Wilson recognized Carranza's forces as the legitimate government of Mexico. Pancho Villa, who had recently suffered devastating losses at the hands of Carranza's army, turned in fury against the United States. After first killing fifteen United States mine officials who were traveling through Chihuahua, Villa then sent his troops across the border into New Mexico, where they murdered eighteen Americans and terrorized the town of Columbus.

In response, President Wilson immediately ordered 6,000 cavalry troops under General John J. Pershing to find Villa, who was long gone by the time Pershing's expedition was organized a week later. Villa was, naturally, protected by his supporters in the north and Pershing's efforts to find him failed. Nevertheless, Pershing remained in Mexico for about ten months, long after Carranza had asked Wilson to withdraw the troops.

Wilson's refusal to withdraw the cavalry when requested, combined with Pancho Villa's popularity, guaranteed that this episode would long remain in the Mexican memory as one more incident of United States interference in Mexico's affairs. Together, the pursuit of Villa and the occupation of Veracruz branded the United States as an interventionist nation that would, when it felt circumstances warranted it, use military power to force its will on Mexico.

These, then, are some of the historical factors that have shaped the attitude of many Mexicans toward the United States. But in considering the elements that come together in Mexico's relationship with its neighbor, it is also necessary to include the present-day reality of Mexican politics—a political climate that is, nonetheless, rooted in the country's revolutionary past.

The Mexican people take great pride in having had the first social revolution of the twentieth century, predating the upheavals in Russia, China, and Cuba, which were inspired by the ideology of Karl Marx. Over the years, the ideals of the Revolution have given the Mexicans a sense of themselves as people who value social justice, and today the government feels a strong responsibility to carry on this tradition.

GOVERNMENT AND POLITICS TODAY

Mexico's present government is, in itself, a part of the nation's revolutionary tradition. From the time of the Revolution, political power has been shared by two groups: one, a social and political elite—made up principally of businessmen, high-level civil servants, and professional people, such as lawyers, doctors, engineers, and accountants; the other, a coalition of leftists comprising intellectuals, union officials, local politicians, peasants, and the urban poor. Today these groups come together in Mexico's dominant political party, the Partido Revolucionario Institucional, commonly known by its acronym, PRI. The PRI is one of Mexico's strongest institutions because the country's president is always chosen from its ranks and during his term of office he serves as the party's leader.

The Mexican political system is democratic to the extent that the president and members of the Congress are elected by the people. And because the president cannot be reelected, he cannot become a self-perpetuating, personal dictator.

The system, however, has been described as a "limited democracy" because it has many characteristics of an authoritarian government. The president, for example, runs for election without meaningful opposition, and through the power to veto all legislation, he controls the Congress. He also exercises complete control over the government bureaucracy, the courts, and the PRI. Customarily, there is no criticism of the president's policies and decisions while he is in office, and toward the end of his six-year term he chooses his successor from the PRI. Yet for all that it may lack as a true democracy, this system of government has given Mexico more than fifty years of political stability. This fact can be attributed in large measure to the PRI's ability to convert those who would challenge its authority into supporters of the party and government. This process, called co-optation, is an important aspect of Mexican political life.

ACCOMMODATING DISSIDENTS

Since the time of the Revolution, Mexico's leaders have tried to bring potential dissidents into the political fold by offering them benefits in return for their support. These benefits have taken the form of land for peasants, higher wages for workers, social services for the urban poor, and political favors for the middle class. Sometimes the concessions offered to would-be opponents are more symbolic than real. As an example, in recognition of the importance of radical leftists in Mexican political life, all politicians incorporate revolutionary ideology in their speeches and writings. But they can speak with the rhetoric of the left—often including anti–United States sentiment—at the same time they are pursuing very capitalistic economic policies.

Of course, not all political dissidents are willing to abide by the rules of co-optation. When political activism goes beyond what the government feels is an acceptable limit, officials will use force to establish their control. Leftist students who rioted in Mexico City in 1968 felt both sides of the co-optation process. Several students were taken into the PRI and launched on successful political careers; another three hundred students were killed when police moved to quell the rebellion. More recently, the human rights organization Amnesty International has documented instances of "irregular arrests," torture, and criminal charges brought against people for trade union and peasant activities not sanctioned by the government.

Mexico, nevertheless, has seen far less violence and less repression than many countries of Latin America, and under President José López Portillo, who served from 1976 to 1982, the country took important steps to open the political process to opponents of the PRI. This political reform makes it possible now for more parties to participate in elections and allots to opposition parties one-quarter of the four hundred seats in Congress. It also allows opposition parties the opportunity to express their views more openly through public demonstrations and the media.

The reform law has resulted in the development of a number of parties on the left, including the legalization of Mexico's Communist Party. It has also strengthened Mexico's most conservative faction, the Partido de Acción Nacional, PAN, a party that has been allowed for many years. Given the general concern over leftist activities in Latin America, it is interesting to note that the conservative PAN polled 14 percent of the vote in the 1982 presidential election, in contrast to the Communist Party's 6 percent. Still, the opposition parties do not pose a real threat to the PRI, and some analysts feel that legalizing so many parties was designed intentionally to divide the opposition, thereby weakening it.

Throughout their shared history, relations between Mexico and the United States have been dominated by one inescapable fact: since the mid-nineteenth century, Mexico's size and wealth have never approached those of the United States. At the beginning of the twentieth century, the United States was on the way to becoming an industrial giant; Mexico was still a poor country laboring toward economic development against considerable odds. Today, in spite of its enormous progress, Mexico remains a newly industrialized country living next door to the leading industrial power of the Western world.

CHAPTER 3

THE UNITED STATES PERSPECTIVE

From the earliest days of the United States until well into the twentieth century, many ordinary citizens and government officials were guilty of an attitude of superiority over their southern neighbors. This attitude, which still exists in some quarters in the 1980s, had its origins centuries ago in the rivalry between England and Spain for the domination of Europe. From the sixteenth century, the English perpetuated an image of their Spanish enemies as untrustworthy, cruel, and tyrannical—a stereotype that came to the New World with the English colonists and flourished. Along with independence from Spain, Mexicans inherited the cultural stereotype that had attached itself to their colonial masters, and the political disorder that followed Mexican independence convinced North Americans that the Mexicans were incapable of self-government. Soon economic forces were contributing even further to the North American's now well-entrenched belief in his superiority.

The United States and Mexico began their lives as independent nations at roughly the same territorial size and population. By the middle of the nineteenth century, however, a gap in economic development had opened that could seemingly never be closed. For Mexico, independence brought political disorder that created a bad climate for economic progress; in the United States, on the other hand, years of political stability after independence made possible the growth of manufacturing and shipping industries.

In 1848, the terms of the Treaty of Guadalupe Hidalgo vastly increased the territory of the United States, making it four times as large as Mexico and giving the United States the additional advantage of size. Its productive land was greater than that of Mexico's, its climate more varied and suited to agriculture. Forests, rivers, and mineral resources were available in abundance. As Americans went about the business of building their nation, they not only felt culturally superior to their Mexican neighbors, they had the economic muscle to back up the belief.

It was, in fact, this belief in American superiority—embodied in the idea that it was America's "manifest destiny" to extend its territory to the Pacific Ocean—that had sent U.S. troops to war with Mexico in 1846. But the United States had long felt politically superior to the other nations in the Western Hemisphere.

As the first New World colony to rebel against a European monarch, the United States had early come to see itself as the protector of democracy in the hemisphere. To counter the possibility of an attempt by Spain and its allies to recover its newly liberated colonies in Mexico and South America, the United States stepped in to defend the cherished American values of independence and government by the people. In his 1823 State of the Union address, President James Monroe announced the doctrine that bears his name:

> We owe it therefore to candor, and to the amicable relations existing between the United States and those [European] powers, to declare that we should consider any attempt on their part to extend their system to any portions of this hemisphere as dangerous to our peace and safety.

At the same time that the Monroe Doctrine defended independence and representative government in the Americas, it also established the United States' own sphere of influence in the hemisphere. Some eighty years after the declaration of the Monroe Doctrine, President Theodore Roosevelt added his "corollary," stating that

A cartoon of the 1870s demonstrates Uncle Sam's high-handed attitude toward neighbors to the south.

the United States would use military force when necessary to protect its interests within that sphere of influence. Although the United States would not tolerate foreign intervention in the hemisphere, intervention by the United States had official approval.

For more than a century, the concept of "manifest destiny" and the principles of the Monroe Doctrine and the Roosevelt Corollary guided United States dealings with Latin America. The results of this policy in United States relations with Mexico are evident: an aggressive war that gained territory the United States wanted for its continental expansion; economic domination that served the commercial interests of United States citizens at the expense of Mexico's sovereignty and economic development; and military intervention in the Mexican Revolution. It was an arrogant policy that won the United States few Mexican friends.

THE ARRIVAL OF
THE GOOD NEIGHBOR

The United States outlook toward Mexico began to change in the late 1920s when President Calvin Coolidge appointed Dwight Morrow as U.S. ambassador to Mexico. Unlike past ambassadors, Morrow won the hearts of the Mexican people by enthusiastically embracing their culture, and he established a good working relationship with the Mexican president, Plutarco Calles, through his informal approach to solving problems between the two countries.

The progress toward better relations begun under Coolidge came to full flower during the administration of Franklin D. Roosevelt when FDR's "Good Neighbor Policy" signaled an important change in United States relations with all Latin-American countries and with Mexico in particular. With the Good Neighbor Policy the United States accepted the principle of nonintervention in the internal affairs of other American nations and established a policy of respect for their national sovereignty.

But any policy is only as good as the actions that implement it. The success of the Good Neighbor Policy came from the fact that it worked when put into practice. In the economic sphere, Mexico had occasion to test the sincerity of its "good neighbor" when President Lázaro Cárdenas nationalized Mexican oil, putting ownership in the hands of the state.

The Mexican constitution of 1917 expressly forbade foreign ownership of land and foreign exploitation of minerals, unless the right was granted by the Mexican government. Through the 1920s and well into the 1930s, the courts allowed foreign oil companies, many of them owned by Americans, to operate with minimal restrictions in return for their recognition of Mexico's legal sovereignty over its resources. Then in 1936, a strike by Mexican oil workers led to an evaluation of their grievances against their American employers. An official arbitration board decided in favor of the workers: the oil companies must raise workers' wages and provide better systems for pensions and social welfare. The oil companies, however, refused to comply with the order because the measures would be too costly.

In the end, the response of the Mexican president Lázaro Cárdenas proved far more costly to the oil companies than raising workers' wages. On March 18, 1938, Cárdenas expropriated the holdings of all foreign oil companies.

In an earlier time, the United States government might have responded by sending troops to protect the rights and property of its citizens. In 1938, however, President Roosevelt and Secretary of State Cordell Hull followed the Good Neighbor Policy, supporting Mexico's sovereign right to nationalize its oil. They concentrated their attention on the difficult task of negotiating terms of compensation for the oil companies' losses.

In 1943, Franklin Roosevelt became the first U.S. president to make an official state visit to Mexico, underscoring the value the United States placed on Mexico as an ally in World War II. Throughout the war, Mexico helped the military effort by supplying important strategic raw materials to United States industries. Mexican soldiers fought in the U.S. Army, and a squadron of the newly organized Mexican Air Force saw action in the Pacific in 1945. On the home front, Mexico's Bracero Program provided Mexican workers for jobs left vacant by U.S. servicemen in the areas of agriculture and transportation.

The Good Neighbor Policy laid the groundwork for the "era of good feeling"—a period of roughly twenty years when Mexico–United States relations were marked by cordiality, mutual support, and dedication to resolving the problems that arose between the two countries. It was during this time that the idea of a partnership between the neighbors took root, and it was also at this time that the personal relationship between the leaders of the two countries became a significant factor in their relations. In the 1960s and 1970s, however, world events, and especially events in the Western Hemisphere, began to cause an erosion in United States relations with Mexico.

THE THREAT FROM THE LEFT

Fidel Castro's revolution in Cuba in 1959 officially brought Communism to the Western Hemisphere—and not only to the hemisphere, but to the United States' own backyard, just ninety miles away from Florida. When Castro announced in 1961 that he was a Communist and that he would look to the Soviet Union for economic and military assistance, the United States rallied the nations of Latin America to oppose totalitarianism in the hemisphere. But during this period Mexico was beginning to pursue the independent course in foreign affairs that it has continued to follow to the present time. When the United States led members of the Organization of American States (OAS) in voting to exclude Cuba from the hemispheric organization and to enforce economic sanctions against the Communist state, Mexico refused to follow. Stressing its belief in self-determination for all people, Mexico refused to break diplomatic relations with Cuba, and has maintained a friendly relationship with Castro ever since.

Through the decade of the 1960s and into the early 1970s the United States watched in alarm as leftist rhetoric found increasing tolerance in Mexico. The fact that this rhetoric most often took the form of denunciations of the United States was particularly damaging to relations between the countries. Anti-American sentiment is nothing new in Latin America, but in this period it became identified with extremists who in United States eyes were indistinguishable from Fidel Castro's revolutionaries.

Increasingly, it seemed that even at the official level Mexico was distancing itself from the United States. Luis Echeverría Alvarez, who became Mexico's president in 1970, went even further than his predecessors had done in establishing an independent course for Mexico in foreign affairs. Echeverría sought to make his country a leader in the Third World, and in doing so positioned himself in opposition to the United States on many issues. Echeverría's friendship with Chile's legally elected Marxist president, Salvador Allende, caused particular concern in Washington.

Until Echeverría's presidency, the United States and Mexico had usually managed to keep foreign policy differences separate from the many other issues that affected the two countries. In the early 1960s, for example, at the same time that Mexico was actively opposing United States policy toward Cuba, progress was made in resolving two problems that had long defied solution: the settlement of a hundred-year-old dispute over the Chamizal, a piece of land that had shifted to the U.S. side of the Rio Grande when the river changed course in 1864; and an agreement to begin negotiations on the issue of the quality of water in the Colorado River which is shared by the United States and Mexico.

But the deterioration in relations between the two countries in the 1970s was not limited to disputes over foreign policy and it was difficult to reverse. The relationship reached a low point during the latter years of

Jimmy Carter's administration. Mexico's economy was booming as a result of new discoveries of enormous oil reserves, and this economic strength made it easier than ever for Mexico to pursue an independent course in the world. As a result, disagreements with the United States over agricultural trade, the sale of natural gas, and fishing rights became major irritants. And a multitude of small grievances arose over such things as U.S. ambassadorial appointments and U.S. visitors' visas for Mexican businessmen. Mexico's foreign minister was noted for his anti-American attitudes, and the personal relationship between Presidents Jimmy Carter and José López Portillo was icy.

The election of Ronald Reagan to the U.S. presidency in 1980 saw an improvement at least in the personal aspects of the relationship between the United States and Mexico. It has generally been considered that as a Californian and a former governor of that border state, Reagan brings to his dealings with Mexico a clearer understanding of the Mexican perspective than most U.S. presidents. And, indeed, in recent years both Mexico and the United States have shown a renewed willingness to mend some of the fences that were trampled in the 1970s. With so many issues to discuss—in trade and finance, in foreign affairs, on questions of importance to the border regions—it is imperative that the United States and Mexico continue to look for ways to bridge their differences.

An interesting appraisal of the relationship between the two countries was offered by Professor Bruce M. Bagley of Johns Hopkins University in an article in *Current History* magazine. Professor Bagley believes that the difference between the United States and Mexico often arises from misperceptions of the relationship by United States officials. The United States, he writes, has too often assumed that Mexico's national interests are the same as its own when in fact this is not the case. The United States, for example, assumes that because Mexico supports democracy against totalitarian Communism, it is as concerned as the United States to secure itself against Soviet-Cuban expansion in the hemisphere.

Likewise, their shared border, their similar, capitalist-oriented economic systems, and their close trade links do not necessarily add up to identical interests.

When Mexico's view of its own interests leads it to oppose U.S. policy—as in its refusal to break ties with Cuba, or more recently, its decision to maintain friendly relations with the Sandinista regime in Nicaragua, the United States considers the Mexicans anti-American and ignorant of the extent of Soviet-Cuban influence. This attitude, Professor Bagley concludes, reflects an unwillingness on the part of U.S. politicians to accept the idea that Mexico's interests do not always coincide with those of the United States.

And what exactly are the United States interests in its relations with Mexico? Indeed, they are many and varied. On one point, however, everyone in the United States would agree: it is vitally important to the United States to have an economically and politically stable Mexico on its southern border.

MEXICO'S STRATEGIC IMPORTANCE

The word strategic, in military terms, means having an advantageous position over one's opponent. In the context of hemispheric relations in the 1980s, Mexico's location means that the United States has a strategic interest in ensuring the country's stability as a bulwark against Marxist revolution that might threaten U.S. security.

Throughout the history of the United States and Mexico, the border has remained undefended, and the United States wants to keep it that way. The cost of stationing troops and allocating resources to defend the border would severely strain the nation's military resources and prosperity. But as one of the largest and most important countries in Latin America and the Third World, Mexico's importance to the United States goes far beyond a shared border.

The discovery of Mexico's oil reserves in the 1970s immediately made Mexico a potentially major supplier of oil and natural gas to the United States. The availability of Mexican oil is not only more reliable than that of oil from the troubled Middle East, it is also cheaper since transportation costs for Mexican oil are less than for oil shipped from the Persian Gulf.

Another area of Mexico's importance to the United States is as a trading partner and an outlet for the investment of profits from U.S. businesses. A sound commercial relationship helps strengthen the United States economy and provides a basis for on-going communication between the two countries. Mexico also acts as a source of labor for U.S. farms and industries, and although the problem of undocumented workers is a thorny one, many agricultural producers and manufacturers have come to rely on the Mexican workers to fill low-paying jobs.

Mexico, however, can only serve these important interests of the United States if it remains politically stable and economically healthy. To help Mexico maintain its equilibrium, the United States has tried to develop what it describes as a "special relationship." From the U.S. perspective, the idea behind the special relationship is the interdependence of the two countries, based on their mutual needs: Mexico requires money and technology to develop its industries and expanded markets for its exports—all of which the United States can supply. The United States, in turn, needs oil and natural gas, raw materials, labor, and investment opportunities—all of which Mexico can supply.

On the surface, it would seem a sound enough basis for a partnership between neighbors, but many Mexicans feel that the relationship is necessarily one-sided, or asymmetrical, because the balance of economic power rests so heavily with the United States. In negotiations for fishing rights, trade agreements, and sales of oil and gas, Mexico has felt that the United States expected more concessions from Mexico than it was willing to give in return. Mexicans have described the relationship with the United States as being like a rider and his horse.

The United States has also been criticized for not following a more consistent policy in its relations with

Mexico, a problem that is at least in part inherent in the U.S. political system.

THE COMPLEXITIES OF FEDERALISM

In Mexico's highly centralized government, virtually all decisions on public policy are made by one man—the president. By contrast, in the United States federal system of government, policies toward Mexico are made by a wide variety of departments, agencies, and commissions at the federal, state, regional, and local levels. Issues that arise in trade negotiations, for example, may be handled simultaneously by the Commerce Department, the Treasury Department, and the State Department. And within the State Department, trade issues fall to the economic division, not to the Mexican specialist in the Latin-American bureau. The result is often a lack of coordination in policy goals.

Questions about the quality and use of water shared by both countries provide a good example of the problems the U.S. federal system presents in relations with Mexico. An oil spill from a Mexican well, for example, may threaten beaches in Texas; underground sources of water used by communities on both sides of the border may become polluted from an industrial plant in the United States; a river that supplies water to both countries may decline in quality before each country has received its share of water. In questions such as these—which on the United States side involve government at federal, state, local, and regional levels—who will take the initiative in working toward solutions?

Closely related to the fragmentation of decision-making in the United States federal system is the diversity of views on U.S. policies toward Mexico among various interest groups in the United States. United States relations with Mexico directly affect the daily life of millions of Americans—farmers, workers, businessmen, and average citizens.

Tomato growers in Florida, for example, suffer when Mexican tomatoes flood U.S. markets at prices that reflect the low cost of production in Mexico. Yet consumers benefit by having cheap tomatoes in the supermarket—especially in wintertime when local produce is out of season. Like the agricultural producers, many manufacturers can be adversely affected by competition from Mexican industries and want policies that protect their businesses. But bankers and importers of Mexican goods need a friendly climate in which to do business with Mexico, and they often support policies that favor a Mexican viewpoint—such as leniency on the issue of migrant workers. Union members, on the other hand, feel that illegal Mexican workers threaten their jobs; they want the government to pass laws to control illegal immigration from Mexico. And all these points of view can touch a family planning a vacation in Mexico if differences between the countries' governments over major issues has soured the Mexicans' famous hospitality to North American tourists.

Of the groups with a special interest in Mexico–United States relations, one in particular contributes a unique dimension to the relationship between the two countries: the large and increasingly important population of Mexican Americans.

MEXICAN AMERICANS AND U.S. POLITICS AND POLICY

Numbering close to nine million or 4.5 percent of the population, Mexican Americans constitute the second largest ethnic minority in the United States.*

---

*Throughout the Southwest, people of Mexican heritage have chosen to identify themselves in a variety of ways that reflect their historical experience in the United States, and in recent years, their political outlook. Spanish American, for example, is preferred in New Mexico, and Mexican American in Texas. In California, the name Chicano, which originally embodied a sense of militant pride and youthful defiance, has become universally accepted for all people of Mexican background. In this book the most widely accepted terms, Chicano and Mexican American, are used interchangeably.

Mexican Americans are concentrated in the border states of the Southwest—Texas, California, New Mexico, Arizona, and Colorado—with smaller enclaves scattered in the Midwest, particularly in the Chicago area. Except for Native Americans, people of Mexican heritage are the oldest ethnic group in the United States. They are also one of the newest.

The original Mexican Americans became citizens as a result of the conquest of their country by the United States in 1848. For these people, living mainly as small farmers and sheepherders in the untamed regions of U.S. territory, the westward movement in the second half of the nineteenth century meant the loss of their land to the hundreds of thousands of settlers who flooded the new territory. With the loss of their land, Mexican Americans also lost their political and social power. By 1900, along with many new immigrants from Mexico, they were working primarily in low-paying jobs on farms, in mines, and on the railroads of the southwestern United States.

The native Mexican Americans became indistinguishable from the immigrants and together they became the target of racial prejudice. The "Anglos"—as white, English-speaking Americans were called—believed that Mexican Americans as a group were an inferior people who had no need for good education and certainly no claim to political or social power.

The growth of industry in the early years of the twentieth century drew large numbers of Mexican Americans from rural areas to the cities of the Southwest, and they have remained chiefly urban dwellers who are, in many ways, the poorest of all Americans. They often live in overcrowded, dilapidated housing in neighborhoods that lack basic amenities such as paved roads and streetlights. They have historically been poorly educated and suffer from limited health care that results in a high rate of illness and early death.

Today, however, more and more Mexican Americans are breaking out of the cycle of poverty, and within the Mexican American community there is enormous diversity of family background, economic level, life-style, and attitudes toward both Anglos and their fellow Mexican Americans. The single factor that remains common to almost all Mexican Americans is their use of the Spanish language. While a great many Mexican Americans are fully bilingual in Spanish and English, many others still depend solely on Spanish.

Historically, because of poverty, lack of education, racial prejudice, and discrimination in employment, Mexican Americans have had virtually no political influence. In the wake of the civil rights movements of the 1960s and 1970s that situation began to change. Today Mexican Americans are working together to improve their status. At the same time, the emergence of the border states as an important part of the nation's Sun Belt has brought recognition of Mexican Americans as an important national minority.

By joining with other Hispanic ethnic groups, such as Puerto Ricans and Cubans, Mexican Americans have expanded their influence in national politics even more. Both Republicans and Democrats are well aware that the Hispanic vote could be crucial in Texas, California, and Florida, which together make up one-third of the electoral vote and are therefore critical in a presidential election. As both parties court them, Mexican American voters are growing both in numbers and in political sophistication, and they are electing more and more Mexican Americans to positions of power in the United States Congress, in statehouses, and in city halls.

Some observers have suggested that Mexican Americans have the potential to become an important force in the United States relations with Mexico, much as American Jews have lobbied for a foreign policy that supports Israel. Is it realistic to think that Chicanos could present a forceful lobby for Mexican interests? According to Professor Rodolfo O. de la Garza of the University of Texas, it is highly unlikely. Like most Americans, he says, Chicanos are interested in local and domestic issues—especially economic issues of inflation and unemployment—and are apathetic to foreign affairs, even when the country involved is Mexico.

Furthermore, Professor de la Garza writes, the ability of an ethnic group to influence foreign policy depends not only on its importance as a voting bloc, but on its ability to make financial contributions to political campaigns and to control influential interests such as the labor movement or the media. Few groups, he says, fill these requirements, and Mexican Americans are not among them.

Nevertheless, Chicanos are being appointed to more positions in which they represent national and state governments in talks with Mexican representatives. Officials hope to indicate to Mexico that Chicanos are part of American life, but they also feel that Chicanos bring to their work an extra measure of understanding of Mexican culture.

The recognition that Mexican Americans can make a positive contribution to their government's understanding of Mexico represents a major step forward in official thinking about the United States relations with its neighbor. As pressures on the relationship grow more intense in the 1980s, the United States will increasingly find that old notions and attitudes will not accomplish the goal of building the strong, mutually supportive relationship that officials would hope to have with Mexico. The task will require coordination, imagination, and a much more sympathetic understanding of Mexico's perspective on the relationship than has marked United States policy to date.

CHAPTER 4

FROM BOOM TO BUST

As the 1980s began, Mexico's economic future looked bright. The discovery of vast oil reserves in southeastern Mexico in the mid-1970s held the promise of wealth that might alleviate the desperate poverty that two-thirds of the country's people endured. Buttressed by the money that oil production generates, Mexico's economy was growing at an annual rate of 8 percent in 1981, an enviable rate for a newly industrialized country. For the Mexican people this statistic meant high profits for entrepreneurs, more jobs, more consumer goods, and the expectation of continued prosperity.

The economic boom, however, carried the seeds of disaster. By August 1982, Mexico faced bankruptcy. The government and private businesses alike were deeply in debt to foreign banks and unable to pay even the interest on their loans. The threat of economic collapse stunned the Mexican people and rocked the international banking system. It also raised serious questions about the country's political stability. In a few short months, Mexico's dream of prosperity had come crashing down; the country was entering the period people were beginning to call *la crisis*. How did Mexico's boom turn to bust? The answer begins with oil.

NEW OIL IN THE 1970s

In 1972, Petroleos Mexicanos, PEMEX for short, announced that new deposits of oil had been discovered in the state of Tabasco on the southeastern coast of Mexico. Mexico's state-owned oil industry was on the brink of a renaissance.

News of the Tabasco oil fields was followed by the discovery of even greater quantities of oil off the coast of the neighboring state of Campeche, and in 1979 natural gas fields were located in the northern states of Coahuila and Nuevo León.

By 1982, PEMEX was claiming proven oil reserves of 72 billion barrels, with potential reserves of an estimated 250 billion barrels. Studies released in 1984 indicated that the PEMEX estimates of reserves had been greatly inflated, but in the early 1980s, Mexico was generally considered to rival Saudi Arabia as the world's largest depository of oil. PEMEX lost no time in exploiting its newfound wealth. Within five years after the Campeche discoveries, Mexican wells were pumping 2.5 million barrels of oil daily. By 1981 Mexico had become the fourth largest oil producer in the world, after the Soviet Union, Saudi Arabia, and the United States.

OIL AND THE UNITED STATES

The Mexican oil discovery was good news for the United States. The United States currently imports almost 30 percent of the oil it uses and was elated at the prospect of a new source of this valuable resource that would help reduce its dependence on oil from the Middle East. Since 1978, the United States has purchased over half of Mexico's exported oil and has contracted to buy large quantities of natural gas.

The United States interest in Mexico's oil and natural gas, however, has been a mixed blessing for its neighbor. On the one hand, Mexico has depended heavily on buying from the United States the equipment and technology it needs to extract these resources. In particular, equipment for offshore exploration and drilling has had to be imported from the U.S. companies that control the technology. Selling oil to the United States earns Mexico the dollars necessary to pay for these imports.

Mexico's oil boom of the 1970s was one of the positive aspects of López-Portillo's leadership.

On the other hand, Mexico cannot become dependent solely on the United States as a market for its oil. This position would be neither economically sound nor politically possible. Oil has long been a symbol of Mexican nationalism, and in recent years it has become a focus of political controversy. Mexican nationalists fear any sign of economic dependence on other countries, especially on the United States. Some critics on the political left have argued that Mexico's oil should not be developed at all if it is going to be sold abroad, with the profits benefiting the privileged classes rather than the poor. They believe the oil should remain in the ground until Mexico is able to exploit it without imported technology.

Just as the question of how much oil to sell the United States dominated Mexico's external trade discussions in the late 1970s, so the question of how best to use the money gained from developing Mexico's energy resources dominated domestic policy-making.

USING OIL TO FUEL THE ECONOMY

Mexico's oil boom coincided almost exactly with the six-year presidential term of José López Portillo. When he became president in 1976, López Portillo inherited an economy that was suffering from a high level of government spending which had carried Mexico into a recessionary slump. The country was also experiencing a foretaste of the inflation that would rise to unprecedented heights within six years.

López Portillo feared that to cut back on government spending in the midst of a recession could spark unrest among impoverished peasants and workers who had never shared in Mexico's economic growth. Instead, he proposed an ambitious plan to convert Mexico's oil resources into sustained long-term growth by expanding industrial production.

Economic planning has long been a feature of Mexico's "mixed economy," in which the state controls many industries and exercises strong influence over the private sector, made up of individually owned businesses. In 1979, López Portillo announced his plan for using Mexico's oil wealth. The plan proposed to develop basic industries such as steel and petrochemicals, and to decentralize industry throughout the country in order to create jobs beyond the central region where industry had traditionally been concentrated. López Portillo's plan also called for strengthening the economic infrastructure of the nation by building new roads and bridges, developing improved port facilities, and increasing the amount of electricity generated in the country.

In agricultural policy, López Portillo sought to make Mexico self-sufficient in food production by increasing agricultural output and attempted to address the problems of rural poverty by raising the income of small subsistence farmers who grew barely enough food for their own families. He also established an agency to oversee improvements in education, health care, and nutrition for the peasants.

But the chief way López Portillo planned to distribute the oil wealth among the poor was through the established system of state subsidies. The government had long supported the prices of many consumer goods and services, among them electricity, gasoline, public transportation, and basic foods such as *tortillas*, corn, rice, flour, eggs, bread, condensed milk, coffee, and certain processed foods. By keeping the prices of these items artificially low through state-owned industries and stores, the government had ensured that Mexicans at the lowest economic levels were generally spared the harsh effects of inflation and market fluctuations.

It is widely accepted that this subsidy system helps to control discontent among a large segment of the population that might, with the right leadership, be mobilized against the government. The subsidies, however, are a costly peacekeeper. In 1981, for example, it was reported that the state's 7,500 subsidized stores were running an annual deficit of $250 million, a cost that had to be absorbed by the government every year. And as prices increased with inflation, so did the amount of the deficit.

On the surface, the achievements of López Portillo's presidency were impressive. PEMEX's capacity to refine crude oil doubled and petrochemical production tripled. Steel production rose by 50 percent; the generation of electricity, by 70 percent; and fertilizer production, by 90 percent. Four million jobs were created in the course of industrial expansion, and Mexico did become somewhat less dependent on food imports.

THE CRISIS DEEPENS

Balanced against the economic gains were the negative results of López Portillo's policies. Inflation skyrocketed as the economy became "overheated" with the millions of pesos the oil boom was feeding into it. The abundance of money forced prices higher at a faster rate than increases in workers' wages, which were set by the government. Wealth became concentrated in the hands of the already affluent classes, whose members received high salaries as professionals and executives in the new industries. In short, the economy was growing at a faster pace than the country could tolerate.

The increase in national wealth also brought a rise in corruption at all levels of government and business. Corruption—in the form of bribes and kickbacks both offered and accepted—had always been a feature of Mexican public life, but it reached new heights during the boom years. Many public officials were known to be taking kickbacks in return for granting government contracts; PEMEX officials were reported among the worst offenders. The epidemic of corruption became visible to all when leading politicians, including the president himself, began building palatial estates for themselves, and in the words of one observer, "providing for their retirement."

In the end, however, it was the way in which López Portillo financed the extravagant spending of his administration that brought the boom to an abrupt halt. To pay for his social programs and subsidies, and to implement his industrial development plan quickly, López Portillo relied on borrowing money from foreign banks, using future oil production as collateral. Bankers in Japan, Europe, and the United States, in turn, were eager to lend money to Mexico because they were getting interest rates as high as 17 percent, which meant good profits for their investors. The loans seemed secure, as Mexican oil production continued to increase. And in the unlikely event of a collapse in the economy, the bankers were confident that the United States would come to the rescue. Mexico's foreign debt at the beginning of 1982 stood at approximately $72 billion, of which approximately two-thirds was owed by the state, and one-third by private businesses.

The size of its debt made Mexico vulnerable to pressures both from outside the country, and from within. On the international side, interest rates charged by banks worldwide were climbing in the early 1980s, and a recession in the United States was causing a drop in demand for many Mexican products. The most serious external pressure, however, was something bankers in their rush to lend Mexico money had not foreseen: a glut in the oil market. From early 1981, far more oil was being produced throughout the world than demand warranted. The result was a drop in oil prices. The decline of the oil market cost Mexico $6 billion in 1981 and set the stage for even heavier borrowing from foreign banks. By mid-1982, Mexico's total foreign debt was more than $80 billion.

At the same time, the pressure on Mexico's domestic economy was growing. The high level of government spending was creating an enormous budget deficit for 1982. Inflation, which had averaged 23 percent each year between 1977 and 1980, was pushing ever higher. In the summer of 1982, the inflation rate hit 60 percent on its way to an astronomical 100 percent later that year.

This inflation caused Mexican citizens to lose confidence in the peso because its value was declining rapidly. As people found they could buy fewer goods with their pesos, they began to sell pesos and buy U.S. dollars in order to maintain their purchasing power. This action created a drain on Mexico's foreign exchange reserves.

During the 1982 financial crisis, Mexicans lined up at banks to trade their declining pesos for the American dollar.

Mexico's trade policies were also draining the country's reserve of dollars. In 1982, Mexico spent $11.7 billion more for the goods it imported than it made from its exports. This meant a further loss of the dollars Mexico needed to meet the payments on its foreign debt.

Together, the domestic and international pressures on the peso meant in effect that the government began to run out of dollars. Under these circumstances, it became necessary for the government to devalue the peso, reducing the number of dollars it would exchange for pesos. Because devaluation reduces the value of a currency, it is not undertaken lightly. As it became obvious that the peso would soon have to be devalued, many affluent Mexicans began converting their pesos into U.S. dollars before an announcement of devaluation. And even after López Portillo ordered the peso devalued from 26 to 45 pesos to the dollar in February 1982, this so-called flight of capital continued. It has been estimated that $7 billion in pesos left Mexico in 1982 to be deposited in foreign banks, chiefly in the United States. It is believed that an additional $25 billion was invested by Mexican citizens in real estate in the United States. Faced with an enormous foreign debt and dwindling reserves of foreign currency, Mexico was rapidly building to an economic crisis in the summer of 1982.

LÓPEZ PORTILLO'S FINAL DAYS

To complicate matters further, 1982 was the last year of José López Portillo's six-year term as president. His handpicked successor, Miguel de la Madrid, was waiting in the wings, having been confirmed as president-elect in an election on July 4th. By tradition, however, the president-elect remains silent on matters of public policy until he is sworn in five months later on December 1. Meanwhile, the government is without effective leadership because the outgoing president functions as a lame duck while the country awaits a fresh start with the new administration. For López Portillo, the summer of 1982 became a time to defend his performance as president and to secure his place in history.

Following the victory of the PRI in the July election, López Portillo took a belated step toward reducing government spending. He raised the prices of *tortillas* and bread by 100 percent and the price of gasoline by 50 percent. The intent was to cut the amount of the subsidies that supported these prices, but the measure was too little, too late. In the words of economist William R. Cline of the Institute of International Economics, it was "the spark that ignited the August 1982 financial panic." Writing in the journal, *Foreign Policy*, he described the events that followed the increase in subsidies:

> These measures . . . provoked the public—already shocked by a 60 percent annual inflation rate—frantically to convert pesos to dollars. With sharply declining foreign exchange reserves, the government declared domestic dollar deposits redeemable only in pesos, instituted a dual exchange rate, and temporarily closed the exchange markets. When the market reopened, the peso soared from 70 to 120 per dollar. The financial panic was at full gale.

It was also at this time, in August 1982, that Mexico declared that it could not pay $10 billion in interest coming due on its foreign debt of more than $80 billion. The possibility that Mexico might default, or fail to pay its debt, shook the international banking community. U.S. banks alone, for example, had lent enormous sums to Mexico, with estimates of the amount varying widely between $18 and $34 billion.

Mexico clearly needed help, and it came quickly from several different sources. Mexico's able finance minister, Jesús Silva Herzog, met with foreign bank officials and with representatives of the U.S. Treasury Department and the Federal Reserve Bank and on August 19 announced a package of emergency aid. The United States government had agreed to buy $1 billion in future exports of Mexican farm products. In addition,

Silva Herzog had reached an agreement with one hundred foreign banks for a loan of $1.5 billion to see his country through the immediate crisis.

Mexico applied for additional loans from the International Monetary Fund (IMF), a financial organization with heavy U.S. backing that lends money to developing nations. On November 10, the IMF agreed to give Mexico $3.84 billion over a three-year period, provided the country imposed a stringent austerity program. The IMF required that the Mexican government cut its budget deficit in half by 1983 and reduce it even further by 1985—an objective that could only be achieved through drastic cuts in government spending. Another IMF condition limited foreign borrowing by the government.

The burden of imposing the austerity measures required by the IMF would be left to the new president, Miguel de la Madrid. Throughout the crisis of 1982, López Portillo had refused to take strong, but politically unpopular, steps such as cutting wages of workers in state-owned industries or slashing social programs that might have made his early efforts to control the economy more effective. Many Mexicans did not agree with his decisions and as a result, his reputation declined with Mexico's steadily declining fortunes.

Then, in the last days of his administration, José López Portillo found one last chance to salvage his image. In a move that most analysts considered an attempt to leave his mark on history, López Portillo nationalized Mexico's fifty-nine privately owned banks. Blaming the banks for allowing excessive amounts of money to be taken out of the country, he declared his action was intended to stop the "looting" of Mexico. The government's takeover of the banks was applauded by the political left and by the labor movement, but condemned by private businessmen. Regardless of political outlook, everyone agreed it was the most drastic measure a Mexican president had taken since the nationalization of oil in 1938.

Finally, on December 1, 1982, Miguel de la Madrid took the presidential oath of office, and Mexico began its long, uncertain road toward financial recovery.

CHAPTER 5

BETWEEN AUSTERITY AND RECOVERY

Miguel de la Madrid lost no time in demonstrating his firm control over Mexico's economic crisis. The forty-seven-year-old president was a lawyer whose interest and ability in economics had led him to a position of influence in the Ministry of Finance. His reputation for honesty distinguished him in the Mexican bureaucracy. As president he moved quickly to put his own policies into effect, with the goal of halting and eventually reversing the damage already done.

DE LA MADRID'S AUSTERITY PROGRAM

In his inaugural speech, President de la Madrid outlined a program that was designed to help Mexico meet the requirements the IMF had set as conditions for its loan of more than $3.8 billion. In particular, his plan addressed the need to reduce the government's budget deficit. To accomplish this goal, de la Madrid proposed to decrease drastically the money spent by the government on subsidies and for public works projects. In an effort to control inflation, he also promised increased taxes in the form of a 15 percent "value added tax," a kind of sales tax that would be included in the price of almost everything sold in the country. Other anti-inflation measures included a dramatic increase in prices of products sold through state-owned industries, such as gasoline and electricity, and an increase in interest rates to as much as 70 percent to discourage consumers from buying goods on credit.

At the same time that he acted to bring the domestic economy under control, de la Madrid also took steps to enhance Mexico's position in world trade. He immediately relaxed some of the controls López Portillo had imposed on foreign exchange and declared a new devaluation of the peso to make the prices of Mexican goods more competitive in world markets. The devaluation, however, made it difficult for Mexico to buy goods abroad. This measure, along with a policy limiting imports from other countries, was designed to keep at home the foreign currency Mexico earned from its exports. This money was needed to pay the country's foreign debt.

Altogether these measures added up to a program of unprecedented austerity. People found they had less and less money to spend on fewer and fewer goods. But more important, businesses and industries had little money with which to maintain, let alone to expand, their operations. And like the government, they too faced the consequences of years of borrowing money abroad. Business failures and cutbacks resulted in layoffs and rising unemployment. Workers who still had jobs saw their wages eroded by raging inflation, and those who had managed to put some money away watched their savings dwindle along with their purchasing power. No matter what one called it—austerity, belt tightening, or recession—Mexico's economic hardship was the most severe it had experienced since the revolution.

LIVING WITH HARD TIMES

A few statistics suggest the scope of Mexico's crisis and its impact on people's lives. Between July 1982 and July 1983, consumer prices rose 114 percent; wages increased less than 20 percent. The price of *tortillas* tripled; egg prices doubled. As many as 1.6 million people lost their jobs, and there were 8 percent fewer jobs in the country. Middle-class Mexicans, whose purchasing power helps keep the nation's industry running, could no longer afford to buy consumer goods. A car that cost 360,000 pesos in 1982 cost 800,000 pesos in 1983. As a result, automobile production had dropped 50 percent and iron and steel production was off by 11.5 percent. The manufacture of small appliances such as radios was down 20 percent.

The Mexican people have grown increasingly frustrated and angry as they watch their expectations of prosperity fade before the reality of recession and austerity. Many government officials have feared that hard times would lead to a political crisis as people turned their anger against the government. So far this problem has not materialized, but the possibility of unrest is uppermost in the minds of many Mexican officials.

The government's success in managing discontent is due largely to Mexico's elaborate system of political links, through the PRI. The Confederation of Mexican Workers along with the National Peasant Confederation represent some of the poorest people in Mexican society, but as members of the PRI's coalition of interest groups, they have supported the government. Businessmen of the private sector have generally supported the government because they, in turn, need its help in the crisis. And even the leftists have not pushed their frequent criticism of the government to the point of confrontation because they fear that violence in these times could bring severe repression, or even a takeover by the military or an extreme right-wing group.

One analyst has suggested that the weakness of opposition to the PRI, and by definition to the government, may eventually prove to be the greatest threat to Mexico's political stability because it is hard for people to express their discontent legally and democratically.

Some voters in 1983, however, did find a way to make known their opposition to the austerity program.

When the government, in its austerity move, decided to cut food subsidies in 1983, the price of tortillas tripled.

In an unusual challenge to the PRI that year, the conservative PAN party won five state legislative contests and twelve mayoral races.

One feature of President de la Madrid's administration that has contributed to peace among the population is his campaign for "moral renovation," designed to attack the corruption that had raged out of control during López Portillo's presidency. Because leftist opponents of the government can stir the people with accusations that corrupt politicians have wealth and power and give the people nothing, it was important for de la Madrid to show progress in fighting corruption.

Although the average Mexican is skeptical of the president's ability to enforce a new code of ethics, the people have been encouraged by the arrest of several top officials from López Portillo's administration. Among these officials was the former head of PEMEX, Jorge Díaz Serrano, who was convicted of defrauding PEMEX of $34 million. The imprisonment of Díaz Serrano has helped convince people that de la Madrid is serious about his anticorruption campaign. There are, however, those who will be satisfied with nothing less than the head of López Portillo himself, but for the present the former president is living safely in self-imposed exile in Paris.

The relative calm Mexico has maintained so far should not obscure the fact that many Mexicans are unhappy with the changes President de la Madrid's austerity program has brought to their lives. By 1984, Mexico was beginning to experience long-delayed signs of social unrest and deterioration. Petty crimes such as car theft and robbery had risen sharply. And air pollution and sanitation, which are always problems in Mexico City, had become so bad that doctors were recommending that mothers expose new babies to the outside air gradually in order to build up their tolerance for the contamination. Some observers believe that the right leader could organize into open discussion the discontent that was building among the population.

WHAT MEXICO'S TROUBLES MEAN FOR THE UNITED STATES

While President de la Madrid observes the rising tensions in his country, officials in Washington, too, are keeping a watchful eye on political developments in Mexico. Because of the close ties between the two countries, Mexico's crisis has had repercussions in the United States. Mexico's economic difficulty in paying its foreign debt has affected the U.S. banking system, and its recession has taken a heavy toll on trade with the United States. The local economies of U.S. border towns that depend on trade with their Mexican neighbors have declined, and hard times have brought an increase in Mexican migrants looking for work in the United States. The possibility that the crisis could erupt in violent revolution has caused concern in the United States.

With so much at risk, the United States cannot let Mexico fail. The United States ambassador to Mexico, John Gavin, has described the relationship between the two countries as "a marriage without the possibility of divorce." It was to honor this "marriage" that the United States responded immediately with $12 billion in emergency aid when Mexico faced the prospect of default on its foreign debt in 1982. In addition, the United States government took a leading role in persuading the International Monetary Fund to give Mexico $3.84 billion in credit, and urged U.S. banks to renegotiate Mexico's loans.

As so often happens in its dealings with Mexico, however, the United States has drawn criticism from some Mexicans who viewed the U.S. efforts as unwanted interference in their economic affairs. These critics were particularly alarmed that the United States purchase of $1 billion worth of oil for its strategic reserve would make Mexico the biggest supplier of oil to the United States—a situation the Mexican Left has long opposed.

As the initial debt crisis gave way to the crisis of recession under the government's austerity program, critics condemned the United States for supporting the IMF and its restrictions on public spending. In both Mexico and the United States, analysts expressed the belief that the IMF's demands were too harsh, that they could not be fulfilled without hardships so severe that they would require the government to use force to carry them out. In addition, many Mexicans believed that the United States would try to exploit the crisis to get concessions from Mexico in trade and foreign policy issues.

At the official level, however, there has been little criticism of the United States. President de la Madrid has gone out of his way to say that Mexico's relations with the United States are "very good" and based on "mutual respect." In an interview with *U.S. News & World Report* early in 1984, Mr. de la Madrid said, "There are always many issues to discuss, but I have always found a great willingness on the part of the U.S. to listen to our point of view." In the months and years ahead, officials in both Mexico and the United States will find that maintaining a dialogue is useful, if not essential, to Mexico's recovery from its crisis.

PLANNING FOR THE FUTURE

At the time he took office, Miguel de la Madrid believed Mexico's economy could be turned around within two years. With this aim in mind, in May 1983 he presented his National Development Plan, a program to restore the nation's capacity for healthy economic growth. The plan emphasized the role of the private sector in industrial growth and stressed the need for Mexico to become more self-reliant in its economic development.

The plan recognizes that Mexico's number one problem today is unemployment and makes the creation of new jobs a priority. It is estimated that 50 percent of the

Mexican population is either unemployed or underemployed, meaning that a person has a job but does not earn enough money to live on. In addition, analysts believe that Mexico will need 800,000 new jobs every year until the end of this century just to provide work for the young people entering the labor force for the first time. At this rate, Mexico's industry and agriculture must expand tremendously to maintain even the present level of employment. A large number of unemployed workers could, in time, become a force for political unrest; therefore, the government views the creation of jobs as critical to preserve social and political stability.

The National Development Plan seeks to create these new jobs by increasing the production of basic goods and services such as food, clothing, housing materials, education, health care, and transportation. This strategy would not only provide jobs for large numbers of people but also increase the availability of vital services and locally produced goods for the people.

President de la Madrid has placed great emphasis on the need to decrease Mexico's dependence on imports for its industrial development. Achieving economic self-sufficiency is especially important because it means that Mexican goods will be more competitive in world markets. And Mexico will not have to spend the foreign currency it earns from its exports to buy food, manufactured goods, and technology abroad. In particular the plan targets several industries—the paper and cellulose industries, the production of chemicals and petrochemicals, and the production of steel and other basic metals—as vital to the nation's growth because they are basic to developing other areas of the economy.

At the same time that Mexico attempts to reduce its dependence on imported goods and technology, it is hoping to expand areas of the economy that bring foreign currency into the country. Foreign investment, trade, and tourism have always been key factors in the Mexican economy; in the 1980s they are more important than ever because they offer the means to revive the economy and earn foreign currency. It is in these three areas that Mexico's relations with the United States will play a critical role in its recovery.

FOREIGN INVESTMENT IN MEXICO

With its own industry in decline, Mexico's economy badly needs the infusion of new money it could get from investments by foreign companies. President de la Madrid, however, faces the difficult challenge of restoring enough confidence in Mexico to attract foreign businesses. In his favor is the fact that the private business sectors in both the United States and Mexico have traditionally maintained cordial relations. Nearly 70 percent of all U.S. foreign investment is made in Mexico, and U.S. investors have an interest in more than 3,700 Mexican firms, ranging from auto manufacturers to hotels to book publishers. Mexico's desire to attract even more foreign companies, however, faces some obstacles beyond lack of confidence in the nation's economy.

Under Mexican law, foreigners are permitted to own only 49 percent of most businesses, ensuring that the 51 percent controlling interest remains in Mexican hands. Although President de la Madrid has found room for "flexibility" in the law in order to allow as much as 100 percent foreign ownership of some new companies, foreign businesses would find Mexico a more congenial place to invest if the law were changed. The law could not be repealed, however, without drawing intolerable opposition from nationalists and even some members of the PRI who want Mexican industry and agriculture to remain in Mexican hands.

In spite of the problems, however, Mexico has had some modest success in attracting new foreign investment. Xerox Corporation has invested over $100 million in a new plant and the Sheraton Hotel chain is building five hotels to take advantage of a boom in tourism brought about by the weak peso.

Early in 1984, the Ford Motor Company announced plans to open an automobile assembly plant in Hermosillo in the state of Sonora. Ford will benefit from the low wages Mexico's auto workers receive, and its plant, the second largest automobile factory in Mexico, will provide a boost to the Mexican auto industry.

Along with foreign investment, profitable trade with other nations is a key element in Mexico's economic recovery. Mexico's trade with the United States, in particular, is a matter of great importance in the relationship between the two countries.

TRADING PARTNERS

The importance of commerce in Mexico–United States relations is reflected in the quantity of goods that pass across the border in both directions. The United States is Mexico's largest trading partner, meaning that Mexico exports more goods to the United States and imports more goods from the United States than from any other country. Among the goods Mexico sells to the United States are oil, automobiles, chemicals, and electrical components. Mexican agriculture supplies the United States with coffee, cotton, cattle, tomatoes, strawberries, and other fresh fruits and vegetables.

For its part, the United States exports to Mexico a variety of goods ranging from industrial machinery, iron and steel products, and precision instruments, to corn and other grains that are essential foods in the Mexican diet. The total U.S. trade with Mexico makes it the United States' third largest trading partner after Canada and Japan.

In the wake of its financial troubles, Mexico has an increasing need to expand the export side of its foreign trade. The slump in demand for goods of all sorts within Mexico itself forces industries to look to foreign markets to sell their products. The more Mexico can sell abroad the more its industry will be able to expand, creating jobs and resulting in economic growth at home. And, of course, selling goods abroad earns the foreign currency Mexico needs to pay its foreign debt.

Mexico has two principal goals for developing its exports. First it wants to develop resources other than petroleum and petroleum-based products. Mexico's experience with the oil glut of the early 1980s was a warning of the danger in relying too heavily on that industry.

A second goal for Mexico's trade policy is to develop new markets in countries other than the United States. Those who want to avoid overdependence on the United States for political reasons are especially eager to pursue this goal. But the advantages of trading with the United States—especially the proximity of U.S. markets—will continue to make the United States Mexico's most important trading partner. President de la Madrid, therefore, has taken the position that increasing Mexico's access to U.S. markets is a major factor in Mexico's recovery. There are, however, several problems that complicate trade negotiations between the countries.

One obstacle stems from a basic difference in the way Mexico and the United States approach trading relations. Mexico favors a bilateral, or "two-sided," approach in which Mexico negotiates specific agreements with individual countries. In contrast, the United States prefers a multilateral, or "many-sided," approach. Under this policy, the United States and its trading partners agree on the rules that will govern trade among all of them. For the United States this multilateral trade policy for many years has centered around the General Agreement on Tariffs and Trade (GATT), which has eighty-four members, including several newly industrialized countries such as Brazil and South Korea. Mexico, however, refused to join GATT in 1980, chiefly for political reasons. As a result, Mexico has not been able to benefit from the more liberal trade policies that members of GATT enjoy.

When representatives of the United States and Mexico sit down to discuss their bilateral trade agreements, each country brings its own special problems and domestic concerns to the negotiations. One of the stickiest problems stems from Mexico's policy of subsidizing certain industries that create employment opportunities and encourage production of goods for export. These subsidies take various forms, including low prices for fuel and electricity and favorable interest rates on government loans.

The United States, however, feels that these incentives make the prices of Mexican products unfairly low in the world market. In order to protect its industries against this competition the United States imposes duties on a number of Mexican imports. On the other hand Mexico's own protective tariffs are another obstacle to freer trade with the United States.

As difficult as the problems are, most observers of Mexico–United States relations believe that it is in the interest of the United States to work toward solving the conflicts. Helping Mexico strengthen its economy creates more demand for U.S. goods in Mexico, and gives Mexicans more money to spend. Increasing Mexico's ability to import goods from the United States in turn means jobs for American workers. The U.S. Commerce Department estimates that every $1 billion worth of goods that the United States exports provides employment for 25,000 workers. At that rate, 162,500 American workers could be out of work because Mexican imports from the United States declined by $6.5 billion in 1983.

TOURISM

Tourism is a special aspect of trade between the United States and Mexico that has been a positive factor in the equation. Mexico has long been a mecca for tourists from the United States who delight in exploring a "foreign" country so close to home. Mexico's heritage of Mayan ruins in the Yucatán Peninsula, the historic monuments, parks, and museums of Mexico City, the flavor of Mexican culture in cities such as Taxco and Guadalajara, and the modern beach resorts of Acapulco and Cancún draw millions of tourists to the country each year. In return for the joys of relaxation and the opportunities to learn about a different culture, these tourists leave behind more than 1.5 billion badly needed dollars.

Following the devaluation of the peso in 1982, Mexico's popularity with tourists increased dramatically because the new dollar exchange rate made the country one of the best travel bargains in the world. Tourism rose by 24 percent in the first four months of 1983 and has been one of Mexico's few growth industries since the financial collapse. Officials eagerly encourage its development as a valued source of dollars and it seems certain that U.S. travelers will continue to enjoy the pleasures of Mexican vacations regardless of tensions that may exist between their governments.

LOOKING AHEAD

Two years after Mexico's collapse, economists and bankers are cautiously optimistic about the country's financial future. By 1984, Mexico had increased its foreign currency reserves by $3 billion; its trade surplus of $9.5 billion indicated that the country was selling more goods abroad than it was buying. The government's budget deficit had been reduced to the target level set by the IMF in 1982, leading Jacques de la Rosière, the IMF's managing director, to describe Mexico as a "striking example of how a country making impressive progress toward adjustment is paving the way back to normal access to the financial markets." International bankers agreed. While other Latin-American countries such as Argentina, Brazil, and Bolivia struggled under the burden of their debts to U.S. banks, Mexico won generous terms from international bankers when its debt was restructured in August 1984 to allow repayment over a longer period of time.

Many analysts, however, recognize that restoring the economy to full health is another matter. The inescapable facts were these: in 1984 Mexico still had an inflation rate of between 50 and 60 percent; it was paying only the interest on its debt, not reducing the principal; living standards, especially for the middle class, had fallen significantly; and confidence in Mexico's future had been badly shaken. Speaking of the debt crisis, one Japanese banker was quoted by *The New York Times* as saying, "It will be some years before we do any new deals in Mexico. It will take at least that long for the memory of this experience to wane."

Some economists question whether Mexico will be able to sustain the present austerity program in the face of social and political pressures, particularly when confronted with the problem of an expanding population. The 1960s were "baby boom" years for Mexico, and these young people will be entering the work force up through the end of the century, demanding more jobs than the economy can produce. Increasingly, unemployed and underemployed Mexicans will look north to the United States for jobs that they cannot find at home.

CHAPTER 6

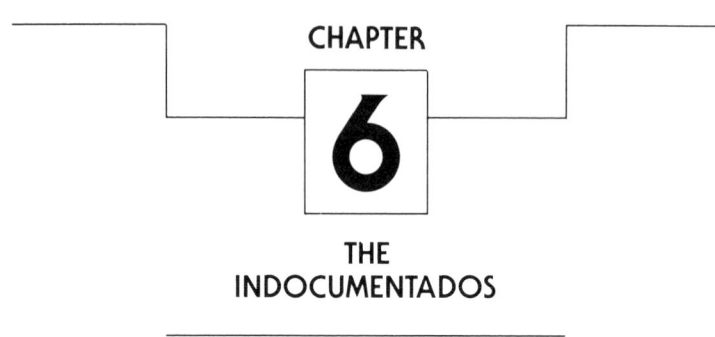

THE INDOCUMENTADOS

Nineteen-year-old Juan Ramirez lives in a dusty village of eight hundred people in the state of Zacatecas, on the northern edge of Mexico's Central Plateau. Juan's father spends most of the year in Los Angeles, California, where he works as a janitor in a large hotel. He tries to visit his family several times a year, but the journey is long and returning to the United States is often a challenge, for Mr. Ramirez does not have papers that would allow him to enter the country legally. Like several million other Mexicans, Mr. Ramirez is an *indocumentado*, an undocumented worker who lives illegally in the United States. For him, the risk is rewarded by the opportunity to find a steady job at wages far higher than he could earn in Mexico. Every month, Mr. Ramirez sends home $300 to suppoort his wife, three daughters and four sons.

    Juan, the oldest son, has been fortunate to find occasional work on a big farming operation near his village, but he knows that opportunities are much brighter across the border. The Ramirez family has been sending men north for almost forty years, since Juan's grandfather first went to work on a Texas ranch as part of the Bracero Program in the 1940s and 1950s. Even now, Juan has heard from an uncle that a rancher in west Texas will be hiring extra hands to shear sheep in the spring. If he's lucky, he might be kept on when the seasonal work is done. As difficult as it is to leave his family, Juan has decided to take his chances in Texas.

    Without the visa necessary to cross the border legally, Juan plans to wade across the shallow, muddy Rio Grande near Del Rio, Texas. If he successfully evades the U.S Border Patrol, Juan, like his father, will soon fade into the underground world of the illegal immigrant. He will become a statistic in a pattern of migration that has stirred a major controversy in the United States and strained its relations with Mexico.

Mexicans have been crossing the border to work in the United States from the early years of the twentieth century. Many have entered legally and become U.S. citizens; others have chosen to return to Mexico because they were not happy with the American life-style. Many other Mexicans, however, have come to the United States illegally—walking across the open desert land into California and Arizona, or wading the Rio Grande to Texas. No one knows how many of these *indocumentados*, undocumented workers, enter the United States from Mexico every year and no one knows how many now live here more or less permanently. Because illegal immigrants live in a shadowy world of fear and lies, it is difficult to count them in a census. And many come and go casually, crossing every day to work at regular jobs in border towns.

The numbers themselves are controversial. Estimates of the number of illegal immigrants are based on the number of people the Border Patrol apprehends, but agents often catch the same person crossing two or more times in one day. A high number of apprehensions may simply indicate that the Border Patrol is working more efficiently. And for every person caught by the Border Patrol, it is estimated that between one and five others make it across—a wide range for estimating the total number of illegal immigrants.

Several facts in the numbers controversy, however, are indisputable:

- The number of people entering the United States illegally is rising at an alarming rate. The U.S. Border Patrol estimates that more than 1.3 million undocumented workers will be apprehended

Suspected illegal aliens are caught trying to climb over a fence from Tijuana, Mexico, into San Ysidro, California.

in 1984, an increase of more than 340,000 since 1982.
- As many as 94 percent of the illegal immigrants coming to the United States today are from Mexico.
- The rise in *indocumentados* is directly linked to Mexico's financial collapse in 1982.

The factors that will continue to push men and women from Mexico toward the United States, however, reach far beyond the present economic crisis to the very core of Mexico's most urgent problem: providing food and jobs for its growing population. The problem illegal immigration poses for Mexico–United States relations begins with Mexico's population explosion.

CONTROLLING POPULATION GROWTH

In the years following World War II, Mexico's population grew at a rate of about 3.5 percent every year, one of the highest rates of growth in the world. As a result, its population doubled between 1950 and 1970. During this time, however, Mexico's economy was growing at an even higher rate than the population and so the country was able to absorb the additional people in its expanding work force.

Far from considering the high rate of population growth a problem, the Mexican government saw it as a way to create more wealth, thereby making Mexico more powerful economically. This official policy was very much attuned to cultural factors that also favored a high rate of growth. The first of these was the concept of *machismo,* the idea of a male-dominated society in which a woman's chief purpose is to be a mother; having many children gives status to both men and women. The second factor was the powerful influence of the Catholic Church, which had long opposed the use of birth control devices for family planning.

By the early 1970s, however, the government realized that if the population continued to grow at its present rate, it would double again between 1970 and 1990; the economy could not possibly keep up with this pace. Led by President Luis Echeverría all the major institutions in Mexico took up the cause of population control. Family planning centers were set up throughout the country to provide women with information, and with free services and birth control devices. A media campaign stressed the idea of responsible parenthood and promoted the image of a small family as the new ideal.

The program has been enormously successful. By 1984, Mexico's annual growth rate had dropped to around 2.5 percent with a target rate of 1.0 percent in the year 2000. Nevertheless, its expanding population will be a major problem for Mexico well into the twenty-first century. Paul R. Ehrlich, a population expert from Stanford University, explained the process of reducing Mexican population growth in his book, *The Golden Door*. According to Professor Ehrlich, a fast growing population such as Mexico's has a large proportion of young people. In the mid-1980s, almost half of Mexico's population is under fifteen years of age, and these young people are only now beginning to come into the work force and start their own families. Says Ehrlich:

> Even if these young people each have much smaller families than their parents did, the next generation will still outnumber the parent generation. Generally it takes three generations for a previously growing population to stop growing after replacement reproduction [0.0 percent growth] has been achieved . . .

Mexico is working hard to control its population, but it will take time to see significant progress. In real terms, this means that Mexico, a country one-fifth the size of the United States, will have to accommodate 110 million people by the end of the century, 35 million more than it was providing for in the mid-1980s.

Closely connected to the problem of the increasing population is the question of how Mexico can feed its people in the coming years.

CRISIS IN RURAL MEXICO

Farming can be an agonizing endeavor in Mexico. Only 36 percent of the land can be cultivated, and soil erosion and lack of water greatly reduce the productivity of the land. As a result Mexico produces a low yield of staple food crops such as corn. A Mexican farmer, for example, can produce just one-quarter of the amount of corn produced on the same size plot by a farmer in the United States.

Factors other than geography also contribute to agricultural inefficiency. For one thing, Mexico's program of land reform in the 1930s divided many large estates, giving small parcels of state-owned land called *ejidos* to the peasants. Today, peasants, or *campesinos,* make up 40 percent of the population in Mexico, yet they hold only one-quarter of the land. For the most part, they cannot afford modern tools, fertilizers, and pesticides that would increase their production. And most important, they lack the water essential to growing any crop because large-scale irrigation projects do not meet the needs of small farmers. The peasants who farm the *ejidos* do not have access to government credit and often have large debts to private creditors who may take the farmers' entire crop as payment on the debt.

For the past forty years, Mexico's development policies have centered on building a strong industrial base, rather than encouraging agricultural expansion. And instead of supporting production of food for domestic consumption, agricultural policy has, for the most part, favored the production of cash crops, those that are sold for export. Wealthy farmers, agribusinessmen, and multinational operations—many financed by United States interests—have benefited from enterprises geared to raising such products as beef cattle, strawberries, lettuce, and tomatoes for export. This policy has resulted in severely limited production of food staples, and Mexico has chosen to import over half the food required to feed its people. If Mexico lacks the foreign currency to buy quantities of staples such as corn and beans, the most basic foods in the Mexican diet, it will find it impossible to provide enough food for the people.

A tragic consequence of Mexico's agricultural policy is the unemployment it has created in rural areas. In spite of some efforts in the early 1970s to increase the amount of land available to peasants, half of Mexico's rural work force remains landless. And many peasants who do have a few hectares of land often find it more profitable to rent their land and hire themselves out as day laborers. These people, then, must rely on finding jobs, usually on large farms. But most of these jobs are seasonal, and mechanization and technology of agribusiness have greatly reduced the number of jobs available for landless workers.

Peasants who are unable to raise enough food for their families or find work as day laborers must search for other ways to ensure their survival. Cities such as Monterrey, Guadalajara, and above all, Mexico City, are magnets for *campesinos* who believe they can only improve their lot by leaving the countryside. More than 500,000 *campesinos* move to Mexico City every year. There, on land outside the city, they set up shelters made of scrap wood, corrugated tin, or cardboard cartons, creating squatters' communities, or *barrios*, that sprawl for miles around the capital. The city provides them with no services for sewage, water, or electricity.

When rural *campesinos* become the urban poor, they become almost completely dependent on the government's food subsidies to enable them to buy the *tortillas* and beans that constitute their daily diet. *Time* magazine reported in June 1983 that four out of ten Mexicans never drink milk and two out of ten never eat meat, eggs, or bread. Malnutrition is as prevalent in the cities as it is in the countryside.

As bad as conditions are in the *barrios*, though, most of the people who live there feel they are better off than they were in the country. Yet increasingly the jobs *campesinos* expect to find in the cities do not materialize. More and more people from the cities, along with unemployed peasants, are looking elsewhere for work.

The forces of population growth, agricultural inefficiency, and unemployment combine to push Mexicans from their own country. But another force is also at work, pulling them toward the United States. This force, in a word, is jobs—jobs as laundry workers and food processors; jobs as maids, garbage collectors, maintenance workers, and gardeners; jobs in small factories and assembly plants, or as day laborers on construction sites. Most of these jobs pay the minimum wage set by the United States government—$3.35 an hour. Mexico's minimum wage is just under $4.00 per day. For many the pull is irresistible.

North of the border, in the United States, meanwhile, illegal workers have become the focus of intense controversy. The issues raised are essentially these: do illegal immigrants fill jobs that would otherwise go to American workers? What are the costs to American society of illegal immigration? How do illegal immigrants affect resident Mexican Americans? To what extent does illegal immigration undermine standards of lawful behavior in the United States?

THE ISSUE OF JOBS

At a time when more than eight million workers in the United States are unemployed, the possibility that illegal immigrants are working in jobs that would otherwise be available to Americans has become an important issue. On one side, the growers and owners of businesses that employ *indocumentados* contend that the unskilled jobs illegal Mexican workers perform are too menial, too boring, or too ill-paying to attract American workers. Some economists agree, saying that if there were suddenly no illegal immigrants to fill these jobs, the jobs would not exist at all. Without cheap labor, they say, employers would invest in automation or relocate to places where cheap labor is still available. Americans, it is suggested, can live better on food stamps and public welfare benefits than they can on the wages paid to illegal workers. According to this view, undocumented workers do not displace Americans. Furthermore, some people argue that the American economy needs unskilled workers in order to grow. They note that where businesses such as small manufacturing or assembly plants are dependent on cheap illegal labor for unskilled work, other middle-income jobs in sales, administration, and accounting are protected for Americans. They point out that unemployment has been low in places such as Florida, Texas, and California, which have large populations of both legal and illegal immigrants.

Opposing this view are other congressmen, journalists, economists, and spokesmen for organized labor who believe that illegal immigrants do take jobs that rightfully belong to American workers. By accepting low wages and poor working conditions, these people say, illegal workers compete unfairly with members of labor unions and also with the poorest Americans—young, unskilled blacks who are looking for their first jobs and constitute the largest group of unemployed in the United States. There is some feeling, too, that the so-called "dirty" jobs that illegal workers do might become less dirty and menial if employers had to hire Americans to fill them. Wages might rise and conditions improve. At the same time, some observers believe that illegal workers are no longer employed solely in such undesirable jobs as dishwashers and building cleaners. According to Donald Huddle, a member of the Texas governor's Task Force on Immigration, one-third of the commercial constructión jobs in Houston are held by undocumented workers earning an average of $4.64 an hour, about $1.30 over the minimum wage.

In addition to the issue of jobs, vigorous opponents of illegal immigration raise another set of questions, revolving around the financial burden illegal immigrants place on American society. How much does it cost the United States to support its population of *indocumentados*?

THE COST TO THE TAXPAYER

The issue of how much illegal immigration costs is complex. The Immigration and Naturalization Service (INS)—the arm of the government responsible for enforcing immigration laws—maintains that illegal workers cost the United States a total of $4 billion in wages, welfare benefits, and lost income taxes. Other groups have put the figure even higher. Additionally experts estimate that the *indocumentados* send $3 billion back to their families every year, taking that money out of the American economy.

On the other side of the issue are those who feel that many undocumented workers contribute their share to the national treasury. According to Paul Ehrlich, three-quarters of all illegals have income tax withheld from their pay at work, and two-thirds to three-quarters pay into the Social Security system. Ehrlich points out that the illegals rarely collect Social Security benefits, and most would qualify for a refund if they filed income tax returns.

In recent years, however, concern has focused on the extent to which illegal workers benefit from a wide range of social services, using forged documents to apply for unemployment insurance, food stamps, Medicaid, and welfare benefits. And the simple fact of an expanding population of poor people strains the resources for education and health care in many local communities.

In 1983, the Supreme Court ruled that states must provide free public education for the children of illegal immigrants. This ruling has had a harsh effect on cities and towns in border states. *Time* magazine reports that

Texas spends about $50 million a year to educate the children of illegal workers, while in California, Los Angeles County alone spends as much as $415 million a year.

Often, the economic burden falls most heavily on Mexican-American communities in the border states. And indeed, the problem of illegal immigration presents a special dilemma for Mexican Americans who have a great deal to lose from illegal immigrants.

THE CONFLICT FOR MEXICAN AMERICANS

Most Mexican Americans have a natural concern for Mexicans who enter the United States illegally, but it is the Mexican Americans themselves who often suffer most in the competition for jobs with *indocumentados*. And their communities often feel the most pressure from the newcomers. For example, in the predominantly Mexican-American border community of Brownsville, Texas, a sizable number of illegal immigrant children in the school population of 30,000 has created a problem of classroom space. The school superintendent, Raúl Besteiro, expressed the feelings of many Mexican Americans in south Texas when he questioned whether Brownsville taxpayers should be required to pay for constructing new classrooms to accommodate those who come to Texas illegally. In an interview with *The New York Times*, Mr. Besteiro said, "We just don't have the resources. We're diluting what little we have to educate these kids from Mexico. It's not fair to the kids in the community."

Mexican Americans also fear that the reaction against great numbers of illegal workers coming from Mexico will increase prejudice and discrimination against all people of Mexican background. In many places, Mexican Americans are just beginning to overcome decades of racial prejudice from Anglo Americans, and they see the controversy over the problem of illegal immigrants as a potential wedge between themselves and the Anglos.

Illegal immigration not only carries the seeds of racial tension; it may also contribute to a decline in American social values.

"A CLIMATE OF LAWLESSNESS"

James Fallows is an editor of *Atlantic Monthly* magazine who spent a year studying immigration. His conclusion, which is shared by many observers, is that whereas legal immigrants contribute richly to the economic and cultural life of the United States, illegal immigration, in Fallows' words, "creates a climate of lawlessness." Writing in *The New York Times*, Fallows described the illegal immigrants as "people who live inside America's borders but outside the protection of its laws—a situation that perverts our economic system and our social ideas." Some victims of this situation are working-class Americans who must accept lower wages because of the unfair competition of illegals; other victims are the illegal workers themselves, for the fact is that the same legal system that can punish them could also protect them against exploitation.

As evidence of this exploitation, border officials have cited instances of slavery and a system of "peonage" under which the illegals are bought by traders who in turn sell them to employers. And many *indocumentados* are exploited by American smugglers who may charge as much as $2,000 each to bring them to the United States.

Another worrisome aspect of the lawlessness that surrounds illegal immigration is the increasing availability of the fraudulent documents—birth certificates, Social Security cards, driver's licenses, and passports—that illegals use to establish false credentials of citizenship. A forger who testified before the Senate Subcommittee on

Investigations stated that as many as five million fraudulent documents may be circulating among illegal immigrants. The subcommittee estimated that the economic impact of these forged documents on government and business may be as high as $24 billion.

In addition to the issues the *indocumentados* raise in the United States, illegal immigration also poses a problem in United States relations with Mexico.

THE MEXICAN VIEW

Mexico has no official policy on the migration of its people to the United States and has generally played down the issue in meetings between Mexican and U.S. officials. Mexico's position is fairly simple and straightforward. Mexico believes that people will naturally move from a poorer country to a richer one when economic conditions at home do not allow them to earn a living. The United States, therefore, should accept the *indocumentados* as the result of living next door to a developing nation. From the Mexican point of view, the solution to the problem lies in raising the level of economic development in its own country. As long as the human rights and the labor rights of its citizens in the United States are respected, Mexico considers the problem basically an American one.

For its part, the United States understands that its open border acts as a kind of safety valve for Mexico's unemployed and underemployed—people who might otherwise become a violent revolutionary force seeking to overturn the Mexican government. But the United States also knows that it cannot welcome all of the world's poor to its shores. To do so would quickly diminish the opportunities and the quality of life that attract people to the United States in the first place. One of the first rights of a sovereign nation is to control its borders, and this is exactly what the United States is attempting to do in the mid-1980s through the enforcement by the

Border Patrol and through landmark legislation to control illegal immigration.

CONTROLLING THE BORDER

The first line of defense against a flood of illegal immigrants is the U.S. Border Patrol, the enforcement arm of the Immigration and Naturalization Service within the Justice Department. The Border Patrol is charged with the responsibility of preventing people from entering the country illegally and apprehending those who are already inside the United States. It has become increasingly involved in preventing the smuggling of large numbers of illegal workers into the United States, and has directed a major effort toward apprehending the smugglers, many of whom are U.S. citizens.

Approximately 2,300 Border Patrol agents are stationed along the Mexican border, with about 300 agents on duty at one time. To help them in their work, the officers use a variety of technological innovations—ground sensors that transmit warnings of illegal entry to control points, low-light television cameras, and infrared viewing devices. This equipment, along with the greatly increased use of helicopter flights, has made the Border Patrol far more efficient in recent years.

Without effective legislation to help control the entry of illegal immigrants, however, the Border Patrol's efforts can never succeed in stopping the flow. This legislation is embodied in the controversial Immigration Control and Reform Act which at this writing is before the Congress. This bill, commonly called the Simpson-Mazzoli bill after its sponsors, Senator Alan K. Simpson, a Wyoming Republican, and Representative Romano L. Mazzoli, a Democrat from Kentucky, represents a major effort to redefine the U.S. immigration laws.

The provisions of the Simpson-Mazzoli bill aimed at controlling illegal immigration are based on the premise that illegal immigrants come to the United States to work. If there were no jobs, presumably they would not come. The bill, therefore, would make it illegal for an employer to hire undocumented workers. The penalty for doing so would be a fine of from $1,000 to $2,000; if the offense is repeated, the employer could go to jail. Recognizing that many illegal immigrants have been living in the United States for a number of years, the bill includes an amnesty provision that would allow some long-term residents to apply for legal status. And a version of the bill passed by the House of Representatives in 1984 also provides for a "guest worker" program, that would allow agricultural producers to hire undocumented workers for seasonal employment if there was a shortage of Americans to do the work.

Few pieces of recent legislation have stirred as much controversy as the Simpson-Mazzoli bill. Political views on the bill have cut across party and ideological lines, and made its passage through the Ninety-eighth Congress extremely rocky. The Republican administration of Ronald Reagan has consistently supported the bill, and has been joined by organized labor and environmentalists—two groups that usually favor the Democratic party on political issues. On the other side of the fence, many conservatives oppose the amnesty provisions and the usually conservative business community opposes the penalties against employers of undocumented workers.

The outspoken opposition of Hispanic citizens, Mexican Americans in particular, has been critical in the consideration of the bill in Congress. Under the proposed legislation they fear that employers would be persuaded not to hire anyone with brown skin rather than risk being penalized for hiring an illegal worker. Yet, as U.S. citizens, Mexican Americans should not be required to prove their identity in order to distinguish themselves from illegal immigrants. The controversy has been fueled further by the fact that verification of citizenship—possibly through the use of an identity card—is anathema to civil libertarians who feel that such cards infringe on individual rights and on the right to privacy.

Not surprisingly, opposition to Simpson-Mazzoli has also come from many Mexicans who are alarmed at the possibility of the United States tightening control over the open border. When the bill was first introduced in the U.S. Congress in 1982, a group of influential businessmen, economists, journalists, scholars, and government officials expressed their deep opposition to the bill in a meeting with the U.S. Ambassador to Mexico, John Gavin. And in 1983, the Mexican Congress broke its traditional silence on the subject of illegal immigration. Mexican legislators voiced their opposition to the Simpson-Mazzoli bill through the influential Hispanic organization, the League of United Latin American Citizens, (LULAC). Arnold Torres, LULAC's executive director, summarized the Mexican view of the bill's economic consequences:

> The bill would mean greater inflation for Mexico and put additional economic pressures on the country. Socially, more people will need assistance, need more services the government cannot provide. This could create potentially great unrest in Mexico.

Despite the fact that Mexico has no official policy on the issue, many Mexicans resent U.S. efforts to control illegal immigration because they believe the United States is dealing unilaterally with an issue that affects both countries. Some U.S. legislators agree. In the Senate debate on the Simpson-Mazzoli bill, Senator Edward M. Kennedy stated:

> It is imperative that we understand that migration is an international issue, and not merely a domestic concern. It will require far greater international cooperation than we have undertaken to date.
>
> This bill is moving forward without adequate consultation by the Executive Branch with our

neighbors. If we are to achieve genuine cooperation we must consult in advance, before changes in our immigration policies are set.

Even as Mexico voices its concern over immigration legislation in the United States, it faces a migration crisis on its own southern border. In recent years, more than 100,000 Indians from Guatemala have fled to Mexico from their homeland, seeking safety from governmental repression. These refugees are victims of the political upheaval that has come to Central America in the 1980s. Their presence in Mexico today suggests the influx of refugees that could crowd into both Mexico and the United States if the present violence in Central America erupted into a full-scale war.

As influential powers in the region, Mexico and the United States share a common interest in finding a solution to the crisis that has engulfed Central America since the late 1970s. Yet the question of how to treat the region's problems has, more than any other current issue, driven a wedge between the two neighbors.

CHAPTER 7

SEARCHING FOR PEACE IN CENTRAL AMERICA

The crisis in Central America was very much on the minds of Presidents Ronald Reagan and Miguel de la Madrid when they met in Washington in May 1984. Greeting the Mexican leader on the South Lawn of the White House, President Reagan spoke of the conflict in his welcoming speech:

> For the United States, the conflagration in Central America appears too close to ignore. Like a fire in one's neighborhood, this threat should be of concern to every nation in the hemisphere. . . . Complicating the situation and making it even more dangerous has been the intervention of a totalitarian coalition which has undermined what we had hoped would be a democratic revolution.

President de la Madrid, too, addressed the issue the following day in a speech before a joint session of the United States Congress:

> We are convinced that the Central American conflict is a result of the economic deficiencies, political backwardness and social injustice that have afflicted the countries of the area. We therefore cannot accept its becoming part of the East-West confrontation, nor can we accept reforms and

structural changes being viewed as a threat to the security of the other countries.

These two statements clearly summarize the sharp difference between the United States and Mexico over the origin and nature of the radical forces seeking social and political change in several Central American countries. For the Reagan administration, these revolutionary movements, supported by the Soviet Union and Cuba, represent a concerted effort to extend Communist influence in the hemisphere; for Mexico, they are the natural reaction of people who have lived too long without economic progress under repressive, conservative governments. In many ways, both Mexico and the United States are correct in their appraisal of the situation. And yet their differing points of view have led them to positions that often seem directly at odds with each other.

A brief tour of events in Nicaragua and El Salvador is essential to understanding the United States and Mexican responses to the crisis.

REVOLUTION IN NICARAGUA

Nicaragua's guerrilla army took its name, Sandinista, from a young army officer, Augusto Sandino, who in 1926 led a nationalist revolt against the Nicaraguan government and against United States marines who had been sent there to stop a civil war. When Sandino's effort failed, the government was taken over by the head of the National Guard, Anastasio "Tacho" Somoza.

With United States support Somoza created a family dynasty that ruled Nicaragua for nearly fifty years. The

In 1984 Miguel de la Madrid and Ronald Reagan continued their meeting to seal friendship between the two nations.

Somozas, however, were ruthless, corrupt, and hungry for power. They acquired vast tracts of Nicaragua's best land, dominated all agricultural enterprise, controlled the nation's industry, and demanded enormous sums in payoffs from foreign companies that wanted to do business in Nicaragua.

Under the Somoza regime, two-thirds of the population lived in extreme poverty, without land and without hope for education. Even the middle and upper classes suffered because the Somozas' tight control over the country did not offer opportunity for advancement or investment.

By 1978, most Nicaraguans had united with the Sandinista guerrillas in opposition to the Somoza regime. In July 1979, after a year of heavy fighting, the Sandinistas succeeded in overthrowing the president, Anastasio Somoza Debayle, and began the task of rebuilding a bankrupt and broken country.

In the beginning, the new Sandinista regime received economic assistance from many countries, including the United States. Its leaders promised to hold elections and uphold the basic rights of a free press, freedom of religion, and the right to a fair trial. Gradually, however, it became evident that the Sandinista leaders did not intend to establish a democratic government.

By 1981, Nicaragua was receiving enormous amounts of aid from Libya and countries of the Soviet bloc—Cuba, East Germany, North Korea, and Vietnam. Much of this aid was directed toward creating in Nicaragua the largest military force in Central America. At the same time, Marxist political influence had come to dominate the five-man *junta*, or group, that ruled the country. Elections were postponed and the press was placed under strict censorship. By 1984 the regime had become increasingly repressive. Criticism of the government was banned entirely; the independent-minded Miskito Indians were persecuted and killed because they did not embrace the revolution; and many political prisoners were being held without charges against them.

The Sandinistas have justified the repression by declaring a state of emergency in the country—a response to counterrevolutionary activity by two distinct armies of anti-Sandinista guerrillas: one based in Honduras on the Nicaraguan border is reportedly made up of former National Guardsmen who were loyal to Somoza; the other, based in Costa Rica, to the south, is led by a former Sandinista leader, Edén Pastora Gómez, who became disillusioned with the direction of the revolution he had been instrumental in creating. Both of these armies are supported by the United States. The Sandinistas have maintained their strength against these opponents, called *contras*, meaning "against" in Spanish, but the fighting between them has threatened to extend the violence to Nicaragua's neighbors, Honduras and Costa Rica.

CIVIL WAR IN EL SALVADOR

Like Nicaragua, El Salvador has a long history of economic disparity, social tension, and abusive government. For decades the economy of this small, densely populated country has been controlled by a few families who owned more than half of El Salvador's land and dominated most of its business and financial life. Until 1979, they also controlled the government through military officers who willingly cooperated with the people who kept them in power.

Any threat—real or imagined—to the interests of the landowners and business leaders was met with resistance. As a result, labor unions remained weak and no meaningful political opposition was permitted. Socialist and Communist parties were prohibited altogether. Election fraud was customary, and justice for accused criminals almost unheard of. Officials used networks of spies to root out suspected "subversives," many of whom became victims of death squads, operated by right-wing groups with full knowledge of the military government.

With open, legal opposition to the establishment blocked, a small number of Salvadorans had for years protested against the government through clandestine guerrilla activities. These leftists grew in strength through the 1970s, until their conflict with the army and with the right-wing death squads reached the level of all-out civil war. In 1980, the various groups of rebels united to form the Farabundo Marti National Liberation Front (FMLN) named after a Salvadoran follower of Augusto Sandino. Under this banner the rebels have continued to fight the army to a virtual standoff, at least militarily. The guerrillas, however, have severely disrupted El Salvador's economy by attacking factories, power stations, and transportation systems, and they consider the military stalemate an advantage because they hope the government will eventually grow weary of the battle.

The government, meanwhile, has been persuaded by the United States to take some steps designed to promote democracy and lessen the possibility of a rebel victory. A program of land reform was begun in 1979 with the goal of putting at least some land in the hands of landless peasants. And by 1984, El Salvador had made a transition to a fully civilian government.

Because United States aid to El Salvador is contingent on evidence that the government is respecting the human rights of the people, the government has made some effort to control the death squads and a United States-sponsored program is aimed at raising the quality of criminal justice in El Salvador. At the same time that the United States has supported these moves toward democratic government and provided extensive economic aid, it has also given large amounts of military aid to buttress the Salvadoran army in its fight against the guerrillas.

THE UNITED STATES MILITARY INVOLVEMENT IN CENTRAL AMERICA

Officially, the United States has pursued a two-pronged policy in Central America, combining military pressure on the guerrilla armies with diplomatic efforts to find peaceful solutions to the problems of the region. From the Mexican point of view, however, the United States has placed far greater emphasis on the military aspects of its policy than on the diplomatic. And in truth, the United States has given extensive military aid to the sides it supports—the Salvadoran government and the Nicaraguan *contras*. President Reagan considers that military assistance serves as "a shield for democratization, economic development, and diplomacy" in the region.

To establish this "shield" in El Salvador, the United States has given more than $330 million in military assistance, trained Salvadoran officers, and stationed fifty-five American military advisers in the country.

In its policy toward Nicaragua, the United States has focused on the belief that the Sandinista regime is supplying arms to the guerrillas in El Salvador. In an effort to stop this flow of weapons the United States has supported the anti-Sandinista *contras* who, it is hoped, will distract the government from arms shipments to protect the regime against the insurgents. The U.S. aid to the *contras* has, for the most part, been provided through the supposedly secret channels of the Central Intelligence Agency, the CIA. But the revelation early in 1984 that the CIA agents had directed anti-Sandinista commandos in mining Nicaraguan ports raised questions about U.S. policy. The mining seemed to many observers to be evidence that the United States is actively working to overthrow the Sandinista government, a charge the Reagan administration has repeatedly denied. Nevertheless, the United States has cut off economic aid to the Sandinista government and drastically reduced the amount of sugar it purchases from Nicaragua. In response to the buildup of military might in Nicaragua by Cuba and the Soviet bloc, the United States has flexed its own military muscle by sending troops on maneuvers or practice exercises off the Nicaraguan coast.

Among the critics of U.S. policy, few have been as consistent and as vocal as Mexico. President de la Madrid has consistently criticized U.S. military actions as intervention in the affairs of another country and expressed his country's fears that the continued use of force by all sides will broaden the conflict. Mexico believes that only diplomatic solutions can bring lasting peace to Central America, and it has taken a leading role in seeking negotiations among the various factions. Since 1983, Mexico's efforts in this direction have been made within the context of what has come to be called the Contadora Process.

THE CONTADORA PROCESS

The diplomatic initiative known as the Contadora Process began in January 1983 when the foreign ministers of Mexico, Venezuela, Colombia, and Panama met on the Panamanian island of Contadora to discuss ways in which they, as a group, might mediate the Central American conflict. The initiative represented an important attempt by Latin countries to resolve what they see as a Latin-American problem.

Representatives of the Contadora countries have continued to meet regularly, frequently including in their meetings the foreign ministers of Nicaragua, El Salvador, Honduras, Guatemala, and Costa Rica. In July 1983, the four Contadora presidents met on the Mexican resort island of Cancún. The proposals they set forth at this meeting embody their goals for bringing stability to Central America within the existing political framework. Specifically, the Contadora group proposed these steps to end the strife:

- an end to arms shipments among the Central American countries and into the region from the outside;
- the removal of all foreign military bases and advisers from the region;
- nonaggression pacts among all the countries to assure their security;
- better communications among leaders in the area;
- the strengthening of democratic political institutions.

The Contadora initiative has been widely approved by governments of Western Europe and Latin America, including Cuba and Nicaragua. In the United States President Reagan, too, has voiced his support for the diplomatic initiatives of Mexico and the Contadora group. In particular, Reagan has endorsed the removal of all foreign military advisers and a freeze on shipments of offensive weapons. He has emphasized, however, that any solution must include all the countries in Central America, and that all agreements must be fully verifiable. Reagan has also placed particular emphasis on the importance of helping opposition groups participate in the political process, encouraging them to use "ballots not bullets."

Mexico, however, has been frustrated by United States unwillingness to talk with representatives of the Sandinista government. President de la Madrid has argued that the United States should give the Sandinistas an opportunity to prove themselves trustworthy. President Reagan, however, has maintained that Nicaragua must stop "exporting revolution" to El Salvador and honor its 1979 pledge to hold free elections. Nicaragua, on the other hand, has insisted that the United States stop supporting the *contras* and end military maneuvers in the area.

For almost two years after its formation, the Contadora group could show few results of its diplomatic efforts. Then in 1984 there were signs of some progress. As a result of talks between President de la Madrid and President Reagan in May, the U.S. secretary of state, George P. Shultz met with Daniel Ortega Saavedra, coordinator of the Sandinista junta. And in September the Contadora group offered a draft treaty designed to move the Central American republics closer to a peaceful settlement of their conflicts. The treaty called on the governments to end their support for guerrilla forces, to offer an amnesty to political opponents, to hold free elections, and to bring an end to foreign military influence in the region. Although the draft treaty has been endorsed by the governments of all five Central American states, including Nicaragua, it is generally considered only a step toward genuine peace in the region. The United States has shown no willingness to accept the treaty in its present form, and, in fact, the dispute arising from Nicaragua's acceptance of the treaty has increased tensions between the two countries.

For the present, it is unlikely that there will be any change in the positions of Mexico and the United States on Central American policy. It is, therefore, important to understand exactly where their differences originated and what they may mean for future relations in the foreign policy arena.

It is possible to unravel the complexities of the issue by dividing the differences between the United States and Mexico into three categories: differences in the way the United States and Mexico perceive the situation in Central America, differences in their political philosophies, and differences in their national interests.

PERCEPTUAL DIFFERENCES

At the heart of the conflict between Mexico and the United States are differing views of the source of Central America's troubles. Mexican analysts consider that revolutionary movements such as the Sandinistas and the FMLN are a healthy move away from the dictators who have long represented the interests of the small but powerful upper classes. According to the Mexican view, the guerrillas represent the majority of the people—the landless peasants and the urban poor—who are caught in a cycle of poverty characterized by malnutrition, inadequate health care, and lack of education. The ideas and aims of social revolution, they contend, easily spark a flame among people who have nothing to lose in the fire.

Few United States officials would deny that the social and economic problems of Central America create a climate in which revolution can flourish. But the Reagan administration has taken the position that the Soviet

A FSLN flag is displayed in Mexico City by some of the thousands of demonstrators protesting U.S involvement in Central America.

Union, largely through its affiliation with Cuba, has promoted and exploited the guerrilla movements in order to extend its influence in the Western Hemisphere. This analysis places Central America's revolutionary trend squarely in the East-West conflict between the United States and the Soviet Union.

To support this view President Reagan points to the massive buildup of Soviet military force in Cuba, where the Soviets have built air and submarine bases and have equipped the Cubans with planes, antiaircraft missiles, and supersonic aircraft capable of carrying nuclear weapons. According to U.S. observers, Cuba in turn has taken an active role in training and supplying arms to revolutionary groups in Central America and the Caribbean Basin. The United States maintains that it is simply balancing Cuban influence with its own military assistance to the Nicaraguan *contras* and the Salvadoran army. The United States perception that revolution in Central America must be viewed in the context of the superpower conflict has far-reaching implications in its philosophical differences with Mexico.

PHILOSOPHICAL DIFFERENCES

Beyond their differences over the origins of the strife in Central America, Mexico and the United States are also split in their basic philosophy of how to treat leftist regimes.

Mexico's attitude toward the leftists in Central America reflects its own revolutionary tradition. Mexico has historically supported movements for radical social change, and sought friendly relations with leftist and Communist regimes. This leftist tendency in foreign policy helps establish Mexico's independence of the United States and gives nationalists an outlet for anti-American sentiment. This is especially important for Mexico's image in Latin America at a time when Mexico and the United States are growing increasingly interdependent in the economic sphere. Yet even when Mexico takes a decidedly anti-American position in foreign affairs, the philosophy behind its policy is remarkably consistent.

In its dealings with all foreign governments, left or right, Mexico follows two inviolable principles: nonintervention in the affairs of other nations and the right of all people to self-determination. These ideals have guided Mexico along an independent path that has often led it to oppose the actions of the United States in Latin America.

Given the judgment that Central America's revolutionary movements are expressions of the people's will, it is not surprising that Mexico considers United States support for the *contras* in Nicaragua and for the army in El Salvador as examples of unwarranted meddling. But it is important to note that Mexico's opposition to outside intervention is not directed solely against the United States. In an interview on American television President de la Madrid said:

> We have made the statement that no power outside the area, whether it be the United States, whether it be Cuba, whether it be the Soviet Union, whether it be any other country, should give help to groups that encourage rebellion in the Central American countries.

The United States, however, often feels that Mexico is too lenient toward leftist revolutionary movements. In the U.S. view, the Mexican philosophy of trying to win over leftist revolutionaries is naive and amounts to appeasing Marxist dictators. United States officials have little faith in the idea of influencing leftist governments, citing Nicaragua as a case in point.

During the first two years of the Sandinista regime, the United States directly and indirectly gave Nicaragua five times as much aid as it had during Somoza's last two years. And the Sandinistas received $1.6 billion in aid from democratic countries and agencies such as the International Monetary Fund and the Inter-American Development Bank. Yet this aid, along with the political support of democracies such as Mexico, has not lessened Communist influence. Far from becoming more democratic, Nicaragua has built up its military forces and become more repressive in its domestic policies. In El Salvador, by contrast, the United States feels it has successfully brought its influence to bear on the views of a conservative government and moderated its policies along more democratic lines.

Ultimately, the United States finds it difficult to go along with Mexico's acceptance of radical change in Central America because of a long-standing belief in the "domino theory." According to this theory, countries in a particular region line up like dominoes, one behind the other. If one country falls to Communism, the others will be infected and fall in rapid succession, right down the line. In Central America, many U.S. analysts believe that Nicaragua represents the first domino; they are determined to prevent the second in El Salvador.

The fear, which is more and more frequently finding expression in the United States, is that Mexico would be the last domino in Central America, falling right on the border of the United States itself. Said one high U.S. official, quoted in *Time* magazine in 1982, "Mexico is the decisive battleground. If we make no headway in El Salvador or in Guatemala in forestalling Marxist-Leninist takeovers, I do not know what the U.S. or anyone could do to prevent Mexico from falling to a similar regime."

For its part, Mexico deeply resents being considered the "last domino." Although some officials admit that Marxists could pose a danger to their country, most Mexicans believe that their revolution in 1917 made them immune to the current forces of radical change. Said Mexico's foreign minister Bernardo Sepúlveda Amor, "We are not in any danger of being polluted in any manner whatsoever by the Central American conflicts." And President de la Madrid has confirmed his belief that Mexico could maintain its stability even in the face of Marxist governments in Central America.

As important as philosophical differences may be in formulating policy, in the end nations generally follow policies that serve their national interests. Yet even neighbors do not always see their interests in quite the same way.

DIFFERENCES OF NATIONAL INTEREST

After all is said and done, it is the strategic importance of the Caribbean Basin that ultimately governs United States policy in Central America. The need to protect its shipping lanes and the Panama Canal against the threat of Soviet bases in Cuba, and the need to defend stability and democracy in countries in the United States' backyard—these are the national interests which the United States seeks to defend in Central America. If the United States had to use its resources to defend against a hostile force in this strategically important area, it would not be so free to meet potential dangers elsewhere in the world—in the Persian Gulf, for instance, or in Europe.

Another concern for United States officials is the possibility of an overwhelming tide of refugees from Central American countries if their governments were destabilized or overthrown by Marxist revolutionaries. Already many Salvadorans have come to the United States to escape the violence in their country and some observers, including President Reagan, have raised the specter of a flood of refugees if the United States does not hold fast in Central America.

Like the United States, Mexico has a vital interest in Central America and the Caribbean Basin. But Mexico's interest is different from that of the United States. Mexico feels that its national security—both economic and political—is directly threatened by instability in the region. Mexico believes that by taking an active role in the regional economy it can contribute to prosperity and consequently to the political stability of its neighbors. In pursuit of this goal, Mexico has developed trading relations with countries in the region and does not wish to see these relationships disrupted by political unrest.

The most immediate problem Mexico would face from a widening war in Central America is an influx of refugees. Already, Mexico has had a taste of this problem not only from the Guatemalan Indians but also from Salvadoran refugees who have been entering Mexico in increasing numbers. If rebels fleeing their countries use Mexico as a base of operation, Mexico could be drawn deeper into a general conflict. The refugees also take jobs from Mexican citizens and aggravate the volatile political situation that currently exists as Mexico copes with its own economic troubles.

Some analysts, taking an extremely pessimistic view, have suggested that if Mexico were threatened with instability, its military forces, which have long stayed in the background of the country's political life, might gain more power. This development could set the stage for a confrontation between leftists and conservative elements in the government that might lead to violence. Some observers have even seen in this scenario the possibility of a military takeover of Mexico's government.

Clearly, both Mexico and the United States have much to lose from continued violence in Central America and much to gain from a resolution of the conflict. Perhaps the time has come to put to the test these words with which Ronald Reagan welcomed Miguel de la Madrid to the White House in 1984:

> Let me affirm today that the United States will . . . go the extra mile to find peaceful solutions and to protect democracy and independence in the hemisphere.
>
> Cooperation and respect between the United States and Mexico will do much in our efforts to promote peace and improve the standard of living of our people. As adversaries, our horizons would be limited. As friends, equal in each other's eyes and drawing from each other's strength, a universe of opportunity awaits.

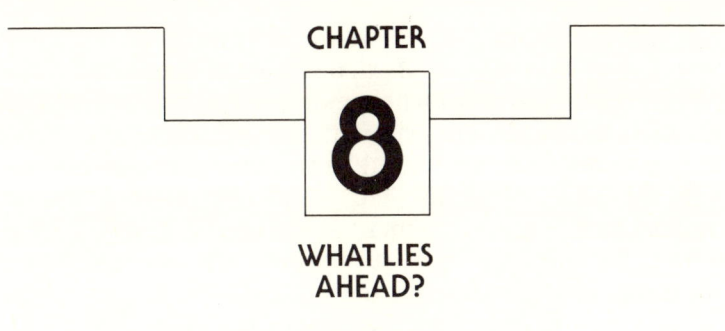

CHAPTER 8

WHAT LIES AHEAD?

Relations between Mexico and the United States have, in the past decade, ranged from the depths of anti-American sentiment during the 1970s to the heights of financial cooperation during Mexico's economic crisis in the 1980s. Today, there seems to be a greater willingness on both sides to accept the differences between the two countries and work at strengthening the areas in which agreement is more easily reached. The inescapable fact that the United States and Mexico need each other today perhaps more than they ever have makes it likely that their governments will make every effort to keep communications open and not allow differences to become exaggerated in ways that could irreparably damage the relationship.

Yet on both sides of the border, national politics can play a crucial role in decisions that affect relations between the neighbors, placing any prediction about the course of the relationship squarely in the realm of speculation. In the United States, members of Congress, who are elected to represent the interests of their constituents, can pass legislation such as immigration reform or protective trade laws that have far-reaching implications for Mexico. And the election of a president from a different political party could bring an entirely different perspective to policies that affect Mexico.

In Mexico, on the other hand, the extent to which the government feels it must placate the views of the political Left can influence its policies toward the United States. For example, if Mexico's present economic difficulties reached a point where extremists were stirring the people against the government, the president might be forced to adopt a vehemently anti-American position to win the support of the left. And of course a major upheaval in the government—whether it resulted in a leftist regime or a rightist military one—would have immense repercussions in the United States.

Assuming, however, that relations remain much as they have been, what does the future hold for the United States and Mexico?

The interdependence of the countries in finance and commerce will remain extremely important to their relationship for two reasons. First, good relations in these areas bring economic rewards to each country; and second, countries that are closely linked through trade have a greater interest in resolving their differences in a spirit of cooperation.

On the financial front, Mexico has won approval among international bankers for its efforts to bring its economy under control. These bankers have a particular interest in restructuring Mexico's debt to make repayment easier. If Mexico failed to pay on its obligations, the world banking system could sustain terrible losses. As late as 1984, a large U.S. bank, Continental Illinois, found itself in serious financial difficulty, in part as a result of Mexico's 1982 debt crisis. At the same time, rising interest rates in the United States directly affect Mexico's ability to pay on its debt. A rise of one percentage point in U.S. interest rates increases by close to $1 billion the interest Mexico must pay on its loan, which currently stands at $87 billion.

Meanwhile, Mexico will continue to press for greater access to United States markets for its imports in order to earn foreign currency to pay its loans. But the United States' own problem of an unfavorable balance of trade, combined with political pressure to protect domestic industries, may frustrate this effort.

The control of illegal immigration is another area where politics will heavily influence U.S. policy in an area that affects Mexico. The outcome of this controversy will depend largely on whether the Simpson-Mazzoli bill is passed by the Congress. Many experts believe, however, that the legislation would have little effect on the steady flow of Mexicans seeking work in the United States. These analysts point out that, like the proposed bill, California has prohibited the hiring of illegal immigrants for several years, with no effect on the numbers of Mexicans coming to the state.

The provision for a "guest worker" program represents an interesting dimension in the legislation that could eventually soothe the feelings of some Mexican labor and peasant groups that strongly oppose the bill. Yet as long as there are jobs and higher wages in the United States and unemployed men and women in Mexico, the issue of the *indocumentados* will continue to be a thorn in the side of Mexico–United States relations. It is unlikely that this issue would be permanently resolved with the passage of the immigration bill.

Nor is the crisis in Central America likely to fade from view in the immediate future, and it is this issue that has created the greatest division in current Mexico–United States relations. With its commitment to finding a peaceful, negotiated solution to the region's problems, Mexico will continue to lead the Contadora countries in urging the United States to accept their proposals for peace. But as long as President Reagan continues to follow the dual policy of exerting both military and diplomatic pressure in the region, he will be open to the criticism of paying only lip service to his endorsement of the Contadora process. The United States position on Central America will be determined by a number of developments in the months and years ahead. To keep up with this constantly changing issue, watch the outcome of Nicaragua's elections currently scheduled for the fall of 1984, the question of U.S. support for the anti-Sandinista *contras,* the progress of El Salvador's civilian government under José Napoleón Duarte and its dealings with the FMLN, as well as shifts in the relationship between Honduras and the United States.

Along with the major conflicts between Mexico and the United States, there are many, many other issues that do not make national headlines. One interesting issue to follow is the efforts of both countries to control the production and traffic of illegal drugs across the border. Another interesting area, especially for those living in border states, is the impact of environmental and economic questions on the daily lives of citizens on both sides of the border. It is particularly useful to consider the changes that have taken place in the border since Mexico's program of austerity went into effect, and what life is like today in these communities where Mexico and the United States meet each other face-to-face.

But the ripples from Mexico–United States relations reach far beyond the border, touching the lives of Mexicans and Americans in the far corners of each country. Mexico's president Miguel de la Madrid has spoken of this interrelationship and its effect on his country's relations with the United States:

> Today, as never before, whatever happens in any part of the planet affects the peoples of all countries. In the case of Mexico and the United States, our proximity gives rise to many and complex relations. Despite our different viewpoints and interests, the inescapable consequence of our diverse social, economic, and cultural backgrounds, the border itself creates ample opportunities for cooperation and exchange that can benefit the two peoples.

The cooperation President de la Madrid envisions can be achieved only if well-informed citizens in both countries continue to work toward mutual respect and understanding. Given the pressures on Mexico and the United States in the 1980s, can we afford to do less?

FOR FURTHER READING

Cline, Howard F. *The United States and Mexico*, Rev. ed. Cambridge, MA: Harvard University Press, 1965. A well-respected work on relations between the United States and Mexico through the early 1960s.

Ehrlich, Paul R., Loy Bilderback and Anne H. Ehrlich. *The Golden Door: Migration, Mexico and the United States*. New York: Ballantine, 1979. An interesting and informative book on all aspects of the migration of undocumented workers from Mexico to the United States.

Grebler, Leo, Joan W. Moore and Ralph C. Guzman. *The Mexican-American People: The Nation's Second Largest Minority*. New York: Free Press, 1970. A definitive study of Mexican Americans, based on a four-year study made at UCLA.

Lewis, Oscar. *The Children of Sanchez: Autobiography of a Mexican Family*. New York: Vintage, 1963. A popular study of a poor family in Mexico City, in which family members tell in their own words the stories of their lives and their experiences.

Meyer, Michael C. and William L. Sherman. *The Course of Mexican History*. New York: Oxford University Press, 1979. A highly readable survey of Mexican history that reflects a sensitivity to the Mexican perspective in its relations with the United States.

Paz, Octavio. *The Labyrinth of Solitude: Life and Thought in Mexico.* New York: Grove, 1961. A penetrating interpretation of Mexico's national character that has become a classic.

Purcell, Susan Kaufman, ed. *Mexico-United States Relations.* Proceedings of the Academy of Political Science. Volume 34, Number 1. New York: Praeger, 1981. A superb collection of articles on many aspects of the relationship between the two countries, written by scholars from both Mexico and the United States.

Ruíz, Ramón Eduardo. *The Great Rebellion: Mexico, 1905-1924.* New York: Norton, 1980. An engrossing study of the Mexican Revolution, including the events leading up to the Revolution in the last years of Porfirio Díaz's regime.

Schmitt, Karl M. *Mexico and the United States, 1821-1973: Conflict and Coexistence.* New York: John Wiley, 1974. A readable survey of Mexico-United States relations that includes interesting material on the early history of the relationship.

INDEX

Allende, Salvador, 28
Amnesty, 76
Amnesty International, 20
Anti-American sentiment, in Mexico, 11, 12, 14, 24, 28

Bagley, Bruce M., 29–30
Banks, Mexican, nationalizing of, 47
Barrios (squatters communities), 68
Besteiro, Raul, 72
Bilingualism, 35. *See also* Mexican Americans
Border patrols, 63, 73, 75. *See also Indocumentados*
Bracero Program, 27, 62
Brownsville, Texas, 72

Calles, President Plutarco, 25
Campeche, oil discoveries in, 38
Campesinos (peasant farmers), 67–69
Cananea mine, strikes at, 13
Cancún, Contadora Process meeting site, 86
Cárdenas, President Lázaro, 26
Caribbean Basin, 90, 93
Carranza, Venustiano, 18
Carter, President Jimmy, 29
Castro, Fidel, 27. *See also* Cuba
Catholicism, in Mexico, 6, 8, 65

Central America, crisis in, 79–86, 88, 90
and United States-Mexican relations, 88–94, 97
Central Intelligence Agency (CIA), in Nicaragua, 85
Chamizal, The, dispute over, 28
Chapultepec Castle, 11
CIA. *See* Central Intelligence Agency
"Climate of lawlessness, A" 73–74
Cline, William R., 46
Colombia, and Contadora Process, 86
Commerce, United States and Mexico, 56–58
Communist Party, 21, 27, 81, 92
Confederation of Mexican Workers, 50
Conquistadores, Spanish, 6
Constitution, Mexico, 27
Contadora Process, 86–88, 97
Continental Illinois Bank, 96
Contras (Nicaraguan), United States support of, 83
Coolidge, President Calvin, 25
Corruption, in Mexico, 42
Costa Rica, 83, 86
Criollos (upper classes), 8
Cuba, 27, 82
  aid to Nicaragua, 85

[101]

Cuba (*continued*)
 and Central America, 81, 90
 Soviet bases in, 93
 ties with Mexico, 30
 and United States, 28
de la Garza, Rodolfo O., 35–36
de la Madrid, President Miguel, 3, 45, 47, 94
 and Central America, 79–81
 and Contadora Process, 87
 and future relations with U.S., 98
 inauguration of, 1
 National Development Plan of, 54–56
 presidency of, 48–61
 regarding U.S. in Central America, 85–86, 91
de la Rosière, Jacques, 60
Devaluation of the peso, 60
Díaz, Porfirio, 8, 12–14
Díaz Serrano, Jorge, 52
Dissidents, in Mexico, 20–21
"Domino theory" (U.S.), 92
Drugs, illegal, 98
Duarte, José Napoleón, 98

East Germany, 82
Echeverría Alvarez, President Luis, 28, 66
Economic crisis, in Mexico, 53–54
Ehrlich, Paul R., 66
Ejidos (land plots), 67
El Salvador, 2, 83–84, 86, 94
Emperor Maximilian, 12

Fallows, James, 73
Farabundo Martí National Liberation Front (FMLN), 84, 88, 98
Farming, Mexican, 67–69
Federalism, complexities of, 32
FMLN. *See* Farabundo Martí National Liberation Front
Ford Motor Company, in Mexico, 57
Foreign investment, in Mexico, 56–57
Fraudulent documents, for *indocumentados*, 73

Gadsden, James, 11*n*
GATT. *See* General Agreements on Tariffs and Trade
Gavin, John (U.S. Ambassador), 53, 77
General Agreement on Tariffs and Trade (GATT), 58
Golden Door, The (Ehrlich), 66
"Good neighbor policy," 25–27
Greene, William L., 13, 14
Guadalajara, 68
Guadalupe Hidalgo, Treaty of, 11, 23
Guatemala, 2, 78, 86
Guatemalan Indians, in Mexico, 94
"Guest worker" program, 76, 97

Hacendados (landowners), 13, 14
Hispanic voters, in U.S., 35
Honduras, 83, 86
Huddle, Donald, 70
Huerta, General Victoriano, 15, 16
Hull, Cordell (Secretary of State), 26

Identity cards, for Mexicans, 76
Illegal border crossings, 62, 78, 97. *See also Indocumentados*
Illegal migrant workers. *See Indocumentados*
IMF. *See* International Monetary Fund
Immigration Control and Reform Act, 75, 78, 97
Immigration and Naturalization Service (INS), 71, 75
Indocumentados, 62–78, 97
 education of, 71–72
 fraudulent documents of, 73
 Mexican attitude toward, 74–75

[102]

Indocumentados (continued)
   strain on U.S. economy, 71
Inflation, under Portillo, 40, 43
INS. *See* Immigration and Naturalization Service
Inter-American Development Bank, 91
International Monetary Fund, 47, 53, 54, 91

Jobs, taken by *indocumentados*, 69–71
Juarez, Benito, 12
Junta, in Nicaragua, 82

Kennedy, Senator Edward M., 77–78

League of United Latin American Citizens (LULAC), 77
Leftists
   in Central America, 90–92
   in Mexico, 20–21
Libya, aid to Nicaragua from, 82
"Limited democracy" political system, 19
López Portillo, President José, 20, 21, 40–47
LULAC. *See* League of United Latin American Citizens

Madero, Francisco I., 15
Malnutrition, in Mexico, 68
"Manifest denstiny" theory, 23
Mazzoli, Romano L., 75
Mestizos, 8
Mexican Americans, 33–36
   as illegal immigrants, 72–73
Mexican Revolution (1911–1917), 8–9, 14–19
Mexico
   anti-American sentiment in, 11, 12, 14, 24*i*
   birth rate in, 2
   class structure in, 6, 15
   Communism in, 53–54, 92
   Contadora Process, 86–88, 97
   dependence on U.S., 58
   economy of, 2, 37, 40–41, 48–50, 53–54, 65
   financial collapse (1982), 65
   history of, 6–19
   indocumentados from, 62–78, 97
   1980s in, 37, 95–98
   political system of, 19, 77
Mexico City, 3, 52, 68
"Mexico for the Mexicans," 14–19
Migrant workers, 53. *See also Indocumentados*
Miskito Indians, in Nicaragua, 82
Monroe, James, 23, 25
Monroe Doctrine, 23, 25
Monterrey, 68
Morrow, Dwight, 25

National Development Plan, 54–56
National interests, U.S. and Mexico, 93–94
National Peasant Confederation, 50
New Spain, 6
Nicaragua, 81–83, 85, 86
   Sandinista regime of, 2, 30
Niños Héroes, 11
North Korea, 82

OAS. *See* Organization of American States
Oil Industry, in Mexico
   economics of, 40–42
   effect on U.S., 38–40
   glut in, 58
   reserves in, 29–31
   state owned, 37–38
Organization of American States, 27
Ortega Saavedra, Daniel, 87

PAN. *See* Partido de Acción Nacional
Panama, and Contadora Process, 86

[103]

Panama Canal, 93
Partido de Acción Nacional (PAN), 19, 21, 52
Partido Revolucionario Institucional (PRI), 19, 20, 21, 46, 50
Pastora Gómez, Edén, 83
PEMEX. See Petroleos Mexicanos
Pershing, General John, 18
Petroleos Mexicanos (PEMEX), 37, 38, 42, 52
Polk, President James J., 10
Population, in Mexico, 65–67
Porfiriato, The, 12–14

Racial tension, 72–73
Reagan, President Ronald, 3, 29, 76, 79, 74
 and military aid to Central America, 85, 88, 90
Refugees, in Mexico, 94
Rio Grande, naval blockade of, 10
Roosevelt, President Franklin D., 25–26
Roosevelt, President Theodore, 23–24
Roosevelt Corollary, 25

Sandinistas (Nicaraguan), 2, 30, 81–83, 87, 88, 91
Sandino, Augusto, 84
Scott, General Winfield, 10
Sepúlveda Amor, Bernardo, 92
Sheraton Hotel chain, 56
Shultz, George P., 87
Silva Herzog, Jesús, 46, 47
Simpson, Alan K., 75
Simpson-Mazzoli Bill, 75–78, 97
Somoza Debayle, Anastasio "Tacho," 2, 81–82
Somoza regime, 81–83, 91
Soviet Union. See Union of Soviet Socialist Republics
Spanish Colonial period, 6, 8
State subsidy system, 41–42, 59

Task Force on Immigration (Texas), 70
Taylor, General Zachary, 10
Third World concept, 28
Torres, Arnold, 77
Tourism, in Mexico, 59–60
Trade policies, U.S. and Mexico, 45, 57–59

Undocumented workers. See Indocumentados
Unemployment, in Mexico, 54–55
Union of Soviet Socialist Republics (U.S.S.R.), 81, 82, 88, 90, 95
 and bases in Cuba, 93
United States
 border patrols of, 2
 and Contras in Nicaragua, 33
 interventionists in Mexico, 1–18
 policy in Central America, 84–86
 policy in Cuba, 28
 role in Mexican economy, 12–13
 superior attitude of, 23
 See also Mexico
United States, and Mexico, 1–18, 28–29
 future of relations, 95–98
 racial tensions between, 72–73
 strategic relationship, 30–32

Venezuela, and Contadora Process, 86
Veracruz, 10, 11, 16, 18
Vietnam, 82

War of 1846–1848, 8–11
Water rights, shared, 32
Wilson, Woodrow, 15–16, 18

Xerox Corporation, in Mexico, 56